S0-BNC-168

IN CELEBRATION . . .

Anne Blinks in her studio. *Photo, Terry Gritton.*

IN CELEBRATION OF THE CURIOUS MIND

A *Festschrift* to honor Anne Blinks
on her 80th birthday

edited by
Nora Rogers & Martha Stanley

AMERICAN CRAFT COUNCIL
LIBRARY

Acknowledgements

Special thanks go to Barbara Conklin for facilitating the posthumous article by Junius Bird; to Lloyd Rule, photographer of the Denver Art Museum and his staff for accommodating our tight deadlines in more than one instance; to Lillian Elliott, Pat Hickman and Linda Ligon for strong encouragement and assistance through all stages of preparation and compilation; to Lillian Elliott for designing the cover, Allen Deyo for the cover photographs and Terry Gritton for the frontispiece photograph. Thanks go to Anne for her cooperation and controlled curiosity about the progress of the *Festschrift*.

Cover: *Replica, made by Anne Blinks, of wristlet woven by Mayoruna Indians of upper Amazon Basin, Peru. Photo: Allen Deyo, Design: Lillian Elliott.*

Copyright ©1983
Interweave Press, Inc.
306 North Washington Avenue
Loveland, Colorado 80537

All rights reserved.

Library of Congress Catalog Number 83-80123.
ISBN: 0-934026-11-4.

Table of Contents

Color plates I and II .... ii, iii

About the Contributors iv

Introduction v

Color plates III and IV .... vi, vii

An Old Peruvian Gourd ix

A Matched Pair of Archaeological Looms From Peru 1
    Junius B. Bird

Some Rush Mats With Warp Movement as Patterning 9
    Nora Rogers

Faugustino's Family: Knitters, Weavers and Spinners on the Island of Taquile, Peru ... 21
    Mary Frame

Turkish Needlelace: *Oya* 35
    Pat Hickman

Reserved Shed Pebble Weave in Peru 43
    Ed M. Franquemont

Derivative Work Based on Porcupine Quill Embroidery 54
    Virginia Isham Harvey

Sprang in the Paracas Period of Peru 61
    Mary Elizabeth King

The Bedouin Saha Weave and Its Double Cloth Cousin 68
    Martha Stanley

Braiding In Japan 80
    Mary Dusenbury

In Search of Collapse 103
    Lillian Elliott

On the Naming of Sheep 110
    Anne Blinks

Breeding Sheep for Colored Wool 111
    Joanne Nissen

Thinking of Anne 116
    Lillian Elliott and Pat Hickman

83-0-1195

COLOR PLATE 1

Menomini rush mat, 95″×43″. Photo
courtesy of Denver Art Museum,
Denver, Colorado. Museum
#1939.440. See Rogers, p. 11.

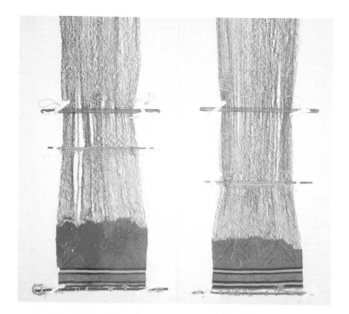

Restored matched looms from Peru.
Photo by W.J. Conklin, courtesy of
the American Museum of Natural
History. See Bird, p. 1.

Winding bobbins for bayeta weaving,
Taquile, Peru. See Frame, p. 24.

Lucio Arechi at work on a pebble
weave band, Huancavelica, Peru,
1978. See Franquemont, p. 46.

About the Contributors

The late JUNIUS BIRD was Curator of South American Archaeology at the American Museum of Natural History, New York. His archaeological finds and analytical studies of ancient textile fragments from Peru led him to become the foremost authority on Peruvian textiles. His influence on archaeology and on weavers has been profound.

A resident of Anthony, Kansas, MARY DUSENBURY's serious focus on Japanese weaving traditions and their evolution grew from several years of study there, and has included writing the primary articles on textiles for a Japanese encyclopedia. Her own weaving has received awards in both Japan and the United States.

Represented in many private and public collections, LILLIAN ELLIOTT's weaving makes remarkable artistic statements. A similar creativity has pervaded her extensive teaching experience. The love of textiles which she and Anne share is equalled only by their mutual fondness for good food.

MARY FRAME, of Vancouver, B.C., received her Masters of Fine Arts, with an Emphasis on Ancient Peruvian Studies, from the University of British Columbia in October 1982. Already her voluminous research in North American, European, and Peruvian museums has formed the basis for considerable teaching and lecturing on Peruvian textiles.

Weaver/archaeologist ED FRANQUEMONT and his wife Chris, an ethnobotanist, spend nearly half their time in field work in remote areas of the Andes. Ed's primary sources for his knowledge of Andean weaving are not archaeological textiles but the weaver/survivors of that rich tradition. While in the United States the Franquemonts reside in Washington, New Hampshire.

VIRGINIA HARVEY, of Whidbey Island, Washington, has been one of the pioneers of the contemporary hand-weavers' movement in this country. She served for years as Curator of Collections, Costume and Textile Study Center, for the School of Home Economics, University of Washington, Seattle. Her books on basketry and macramé are familiar to many.

PAT HICKMAN has taught general textile history at several institutions in the San Francisco Bay area. Her personal interest is in the Middle East, particularly Turkey, where she spent 6 years. In addition to exhibitting her own work, she has also lectured on and curated exhibits of Turkish textiles.

MARY ELIZABETH KING was in the infancy of her career, as a museum assistant at the Textile Museum, when Anne was helping Irene Emery with *The Primary Structures of Fabrics*. She currently is Director of the University Museum and Professor of Anthropology at New Mexico State University in Las Cruces.

JOANNE NISSEN is a spinner and black sheep breeder on land in the Salinas Valley, California, which her family has farmed for four generations. Holder of a commercial pilot's license she also frequently flies Anne to sheep breeder meetings.

NORA ROGERS of Santa Cruz, California, has woven, researched, taught, and lectured on ancient and modern uses of twining, with a current focus on twined textiles of the New World. A fascination with the interrelationship between structure, texture and design originally led her to the study of twining. She and Anne share an avid interest in the role of structure in textiles.

A rug weaver in Watsonville, California, for 14 years, MARTHA STANLEY's studied and serious approach to rug weaving is expressed in her rugs, writing, and teaching. Her structural creativity has been refined and polished by Anne's influence.

This list would not be complete without including LINDA LIGON, the owner and publisher of Interweave Press. Her participation in the *Festschrift* has gone well beyond that of a business venture, and has been as personal and enthusiastic as any of the other contributors.

Introduction

Anne Blinks often refers to her work with textiles as "play", but it is playing by the sophisticated and analytical mind of a woman enamored with problem solving. Her travels have brought her in contact with unusual textiles from many regions, civilizations and historical periods. One by one she has analyzed them, made several trial replicas, and finally discovered the structure and possible original method of production. To this end she corresponds worldwide, comparing notes on fibers, spinning, structure, looms, techniques, and finishing — in short, every aspect of recreating the textile.

Her basic weaving skills were learned in Stockholm with Astri Feist, no mean training for someone who wishes to be a skilled and serious weaver. In part she gathered her knowledge of the structures of textiles while at the Textile Museum in Washington, D.C., assisting Irene Emery with *The Primary Structures of Fabrics*, the definitive book on techniques and structures of textiles. Anne wove many of the examples shown in the book. Since then she has taken a diverse path few have been willing to follow — that of textile scholar and weaver. Most travel one or the other. This straddling of both the study and creation of textiles gives her significant insight that would be impossible otherwise.

February 20th, 1983, is Anne Blinks' 80th birthday. To celebrate that event and to acknowledge publicly Anne's quiet and significant contribution to the world of weaving, its history and accomplishment, this *Festschrift* is published in her honor.

Articles by eleven people appear in this volume. All contributors' paths have crossed with Anne's in significant textile pursuits. Some are handweavers, some artists, some textile scholars, some breeders of black sheep for quality wool. In explaining the *Festschrift*, let us imagine a birthday party with the articles as presents to Anne. Some topics have been offered because of their interest and allure to her, some because she has done so much work in the field herself. We want the book to be for Anne, for her pleasure and amusement. We also think it is a good representation of the diversity and approach which she exemplifies. In that sense it is both for and about Anne. While we consider Anne its primary reader, we hope other readers will gain insight and pleasure from its pages.

We offer this *Festschrift* to Anne and hope it will be a worthy tribute to a dear friend.

Martha Stanley
Nora Rogers

COLOR PLATE 3

Aegean man's headdress, wrapped
with several scarves creating an effect
of layers thick with *oya. Collection
of Kenan Öebel, Istanbul.* See Hickman, p. 40.

A creped silk shirt with needlelace
edging. *Tire Museum Collection,
Turkey.* See Hickman, p. 36 and
Elliott, p. 108.

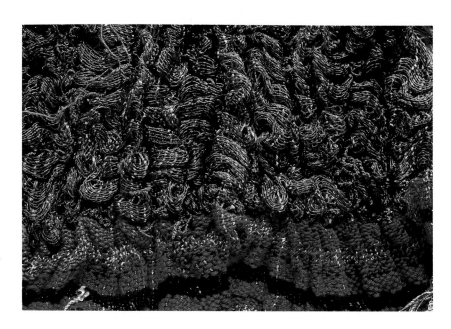

Collapse fabric with metallic yarns
used as weft, multi-colored rayon
warp, overplied yarn spaced one per
inch. See Elliott, p. 109.

Traditional *oya* edging on a scarf.
Collection of Buldan Seka, Berkeley,
California. See Hickman, p. 36.

Photo by Sally Blinks.

AN OLD PERUVIAN GOURD

While the Festschrift is not about Anne, we thought those of you who have not worked and played with her might be interested in one of her "toys".

Several years ago Charles Llewellyn sent her an old Peruvian sling to examine. The braiding work on it was incomplete. And at one end was a piece of gourd. Warps for the unfinished braid were threaded through holes around its perimeter. Wefts of two colors were wrapped horizontally around the vertical warp elements in a stitch akin to stem stitch and soumak.

Just what was the purpose of this gourd section? A number of textile scholars had examined it.

Anne spotted its potential as a shedding device: to order the various warp elements, to present each one in the correct order as its turn comes to be wrapped with the weft. One simply turns the gourd until the correct hole with its warp is up, works the stitch, and rotates the gourd to bring forth the next warp.

Anne has tried it both across her lap (as shown) and radiating away from her, a la backstrapper, as a friend astutely suggested. Anne reports that the former orientation makes it easier to manipulate gourd, warps, and wefts.

We don't *know* how it was utilized by the Peruvians. But the simple directness of this explanation certainly suggests it must be seriously considered.

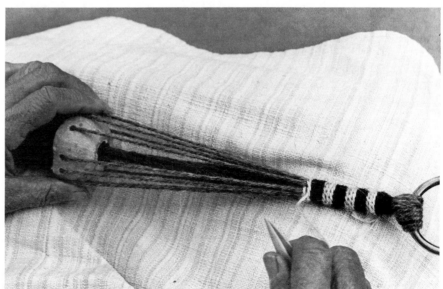

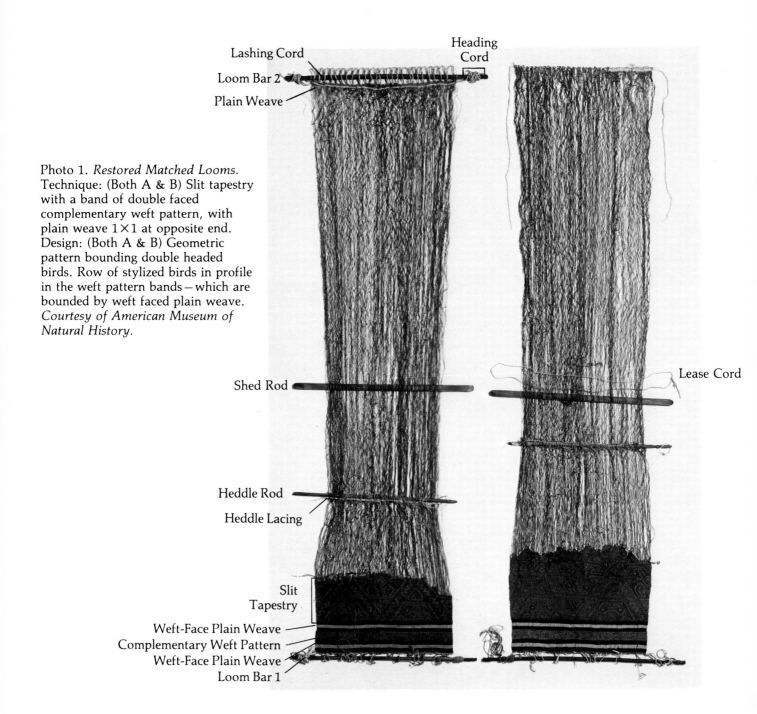

Lashing Cord

Heading Cord

Loom Bar 2

Plain Weave

Photo 1. *Restored Matched Looms.*
Technique: (Both A & B) Slit tapestry
with a band of double faced
complementary weft pattern, with
plain weave 1×1 at opposite end.
Design: (Both A & B) Geometric
pattern bounding double headed
birds. Row of stylized birds in profile
in the weft pattern bands—which are
bounded by weft faced plain weave.
*Courtesy of American Museum of
Natural History.*

Shed Rod

Lease Cord

Heddle Rod

Heddle Lacing

Slit
Tapestry

Weft-Face Plain Weave
Complementary Weft Pattern
Weft-Face Plain Weave
Loom Bar 1

In 1961 a pair of archaeological looms from Peru was given to the Department of Anthropology at the American Museum of Natural History. No provenience data accompanied the looms, but they are probably Late Chancay from the Central Coast of Peru and date to the Late Intermediate Period, approximately A.D. 1000 to 1200.

Dr. Junius Bird meticulously examined the looms and carefully recorded his analysis of the weaving techniques and patterning used, as well as some interpretive comments. Mrs. Milica D. Skinner assisted him with this work, and subsequently cleaned and restored the looms in 1966.

Knowing that Dr. Bird would have liked to be included in a celebration of Anne Blinks, The American Museum of Natural History and the Bird family are pleased to have this manuscript become a part of her Festschrift.

Department of Anthropology
American Museum of Natural History
July 15, 1982

A MATCHED PAIR OF ARCHAEOLOGICAL LOOMS FROM PERU

BY JUNIUS B. BIRD

The products planned and started on these looms were obviously intended to be matched fabrics of the same size and pattern, to be joined together after completion. The function of the finished product is not clear. With just two pieces, they seem hardly adequate for a shirt. If the pattern area was to have been terminated not far beyond the point where work stopped and the balance woven as plain weave they might have served as a loin cloth. A study of completed garments of the period should answer this question.

Steps in production: If we recreate the various steps in setting up and operating these looms, certain puzzling details may be easier to interpret. First we might note that after studying them one feels that the weaving appears to be the work of two individuals, not one. It is difficult to prove what is scarcely more than an impression, but there is a slight difference in the quality of the work.

The recorded measurements of warp length differ by three centimeters. This may be due entirely to the fact that one cannot, or at least should not, put sufficient tension on the warps to stretch them to maximum length. Certainly they were intended to be the same.

At the initial warping both looms had 216 warps and one can assume that the turns were counted. Heading cords were put in place and the warp ends were tied to form loops about the headings at the ends where the regular plain weave was created. We note that there are enough individual differences among the four headings and the similar lease and lashing cords to show that they were not prepared at one time as one single product, then cut into lengths. They could easily be cords that had been made and used for other products. The heddle lacings, as installed, lifted the odd-numbered warps in both cases.

BASIC LOOM DATA

	Loom A	Loom B
Warp length (not stretched full)	107cm	110cm
Number of warps (see discussion)	228	229
Woven areas: loom bar 1		
Width (tapestry areas)	25.5-26cm	25.2-26.3cm
Length completed	15cm	17cm
Woven areas: loom bar 2		
Width (B, mostly disintegrated)	28cm	?
Woven length	.6cm	.8cm
Number of picks	16	14
Warp: brown cotton	∧	∧
Wefts, patterned areas:		
wool, red, black, yellow	/	/
wool, pink, yellow	∧	∧
plain weave at bar 2:		
cotton, white, gray	∧	∧
Heading cord 1, cotton:	∧6/	∧8/
(A-2 tan, 4 white elements)		
(B-4 brown, 4 gray elements)		
Heading cord 2, white cotton:	∧8/	∧6/
Lashing cord 1: (A-4 tan, 1 white; B-white)	∧5/	∧5/
Lashing cord 2: (A-5 tan, 2 white; B-white)	∧7/	∧5/
Heddle lacing (see notes on Restoration, p. 7):		
Two-tone, tan and white cotton	∧	∧
Brown	∧	∧
Lease cord (white cotton)	?	∧6/
Warp group bindings, cotton	—	∧
Substitute loom bars (bobbins?):		
Bar 1 length	35cm	38cm
Bar 2 length	38cm	—

NOTES:

/   a Z-spun yarn
∧   a 2-ply thread with yarns Z-spun and S-plied
∧6/   six 2-ply threads with yarns Z-spun and S-plied, re-plied Z (see Bird and Bellinger, 1954)

The first weaving was done against what we here list as loom bars 2, those away from the weavers during the tapestry weaving. On loom A, 16 picks of gray and white cotton yarns were woven in as 1×1 plain weave. (See Photo 4.) Loom B has 14 picks of only white cotton. Unless these were to have been removed at the end of the work, the ends of the finished pieces would have been visibly quite different from the patterned ends. If they were to be left in place, they suggest that the patterned areas were not intended to run the full length of the warp and that more of the same type of plain weave was planned. Loin cloths often were made in this fashion, hence our suggestion that this may have been the purpose of the finished product.

Once this initial weaving was done, the positions of the shed rods were reversed and work started from the opposite ends. Here the first weft, red woolen yarn, was laid in without tension and beaten down to form weft faced, 1×1 plain weave with the warps completely hidden. Loom A has ten picks of

Photo 2. *Loom A (41.2/5482)*. As
received by the Museum, showing
front face of weaving. *Courtesy of
American Museum of Natural
History.*

Photo 3. *Loom A (41.2/5482)*. After
restoration, showing working face of
weaving—in position for weaver.
*Courtesy of American Museum of
Natural History.*

Photo 4. *Loom A Detail (41.2/5482).* After restoration, showing Loom Bar 2. *Courtesy of American Museum of Natural History.*

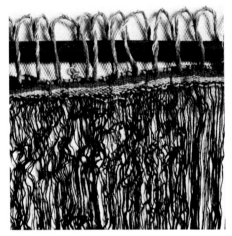

Photo 5. *Loom A Detail (41.2/5482).* After restoration, showing added warps. *Courtesy of American Museum of Natural History.*

this yarn; Loom B, ten. In turn, similar stripes of black, yellow and black were created on both looms, the counts being A 32, 28, 28; B 34, 30, 30.

Above these stripes, work was started on a patterned band. Red and pink weft yarns, working in complementary opposition to each other, were used to create stylized, interlocking bird figures that are pink on one side of the fabric, red on the opposite. It is a design with floats over two and three warps which, if meticulously executed, would have precisely the same number of warps for each detail and repeat, and would involve a specific number of picks to complete. In these cases the numbers of warps between repeats of details vary.

After the pattern stripes were well started, with that on loom A about half completed and that on loom B two-thirds completed, someone decided that each loom should have 12 more warps. Each weaver then took six lengths of yarn, turned them over the heading cord at the upper bar, carried them back over and under the lease and shed rods to loom bar 1 without incorporating them into the initial plain weave. (See Photo 5.) They occur at irregular intervals (see accompanying restoration notes by M.D. Skinner) and at different points on each loom. One assumes that the ends were passed around the lower loom bar, adjusted to the same tension as the rest of the warp, then tied. Pieces of brown yarn were then used to make individual loops about the heddle rod so it would lift the lower strand of each pair and thus incorporate them within the original heddling order.

As work on the weft pattern bands progressed, the new warps on loom A were brought together as pairs and combined with one of the original warps for the balance of the weft pattern row. On loom B they were paired with the adjacent warps until the weft pattern was completed. Once so secured, the exposed lower ends were cut off.

The fact that the new warps did not function individually in the weft pattern shows that there was nothing about the structural requirements of its figures which prompted the insertion of additional warps. This leaves us with only two potential explanations. One, that a slightly wider product was needed, can be ruled out, for on the A loom the width does not increase. The second explanation was that the requirements of warps in the various parts of the design necessitated more warps than originally calculated.

After completion of the weft pattern band, black, yellow and black weft stripes were made to match those below the pattern. At the start of the first black stripes the new warps were separately interwoven. On loom B when this stripe was about half completed, a 13th new warp was added to the left selvedge, this controlled by the shed rod. On the A loom the warps were drawn closely together by the weft, so reasonably straight and parallel selvedges were maintained. On the B loom, less care was given the weft tension and the width increase became quite pronounced as the tapestry was woven.

From the work completed, it is evident that the finished products were to be joined by sewing the right selvedge of the fabric from loom A to the left selvedge of the piece from loom B. The opposite selvedges run through approximately the same place in design but do not fit together as well.

WARP RECORD
The number of warps involved in each design unit at the start of the tapestry weave. (See photographs of looms *after* restoration.)

Underlined numbers indicate location of pink weft; others, red.

Design unit	1a	2a	1b	2b	1c
Counts, Loom A	1 3 9	3 4 3 10 3 8 2 2 2 4 2 2 2 8 3 10 3 4 3	9 3 12 3 9	3 4 3 10 3 8 2 2 2 4 2 2 2 8 3 10 3 4 3	9 3 11
Unit totals	└13┘	└────────78────────┘	└─36─┘	└────────78────────┘	└23┘

Design unit	1c	2c	1d	2d	1e
Counts, Loom B	3 3 8	3 4 3 10 3 8 3 - 10 - 3 8 3 10 3 4 3	8 3 14 3 8	3 4 3 10 3 8 2 2 2 4 2 2 2 8 3 10 3 4 3	8 3 12
Unit totals	└14┘	└────────78────────┘	└─36─┘	└────────78────────┘	└23┘
Tied warp groups		(6)	└─36─┘		

The above record is of course simply a cross section of the [tapestry] pattern structure at one point, the starting line. On loom B it is partially repeated 10.5 cm. from the start of the work.

Note that unit 1a combined with the portion of 1c on the same loom duplicates 1b. The second portion of 1c however, when combined with 1e, does not match 1d because of the added selvedge warp.

The pattern consists of two zigzag zones, a narrow one with a serrated line and a broader unit with bird heads, triangles and diamonds. All are formed of balanced diagonal and horizontal lines. Verticals are limited to the advance of colors along the interwarp slits.

For the narrow zigzag zones only 36 warps are involved at any one point. Weaver A utilized a 9-3-12-3-9 order; weaver B an 8-3-14-3-8 sequence for the same composition. These units are interrupted at the selvedges which are not placed on the centers [of the design units], although there seems no reason why they should not have been placed there. By adding the extra warp at the left selvedge, weaver B imposed her count for the center block on the continuation of the design as it carries over the adjoining selvedge of the A product. This warp, however, increases the total warp count across this section of the design 1c to 37 and would of course add one to each subsequent trans-section count of the pattern crossing the two selvedges.

In the count of the sections of the larger zigzag zones involving 78 warps in all four sections, A has identical ordering (units 2a, 2b). Weaver B used this in unit 2d, but at the center of unit 2c covered ten warps with red and bound them with three covered with pink, instead of alternating the red and pink in the 2-2-2-4-2-2-2 order. As the red and pink provide only slight color contrast, this deviation is scarcely visible except under magnification. Whether there is any correlation between this weaver's willingness to simplify minutiae, her casual handling of selvedges, and her rate of production is a matter of conjecture. One might note in the same vein that there are more knots in her warp, seemingly repairs of breaks occurring during the work.

What prompts attention to such detail and warrants its recording is that these two looms provide a little insight into the planning and execution of matched products. The requirements of the pattern are clearly two groups of 78 warps and two of 36 for each loom. Either there was a simple miscalculation prior to warping or a different pattern was planned. As both looms were set up with 216 passages of warp, it was not a mistake in counting during warping. It is also worth noting that the error was discovered, or the design-plan for the tapestry was changed, some time before they were ready to start that portion of the work. In other words, they were thinking ahead of the task at hand and were involved with simple mathematical calculations.

For some unknown reason coordination between the two weavers was not perfect. While in agreement on the major division of the design, each followed her own breakdown of the lesser division. The operator of loom B went so far as to modify one selvedge by adding a warp in order to balance out her version of the lesser sequence in spite of the fact that this broke the perfect balance for the main theme.

I have neglected to mention in connection with the pattern units that on loom B, white cotton yarns encircle and are tied about warps 51 to 56 inclusive, and warps 93 to 128, counting from the left selvedge. These ties are placed just above the assumed position of the shed rod. When checked against the pattern on the line at which it starts, the 51 to 56 warps correspond to the 2-4-2 group at the center of the 2a pattern unit on loom A. On the B loom, however, there are all red-covered warps at the center of the ten group in unit 2c. As the weaver had not completed a full repeat of this row, we do not know if this loop about warps 51 to 56 was put in place as a reminder to use the 2-4-2 order when the time came to do so.

The brown cord about the 36 warps (numbers 93-128) identifies those warps which form pattern unit 1d.

Photo 6. *Loom B (41.2/5483).* As received by the Museum, showing front face of weaving. *Courtesy of American Museum of Natural History.*

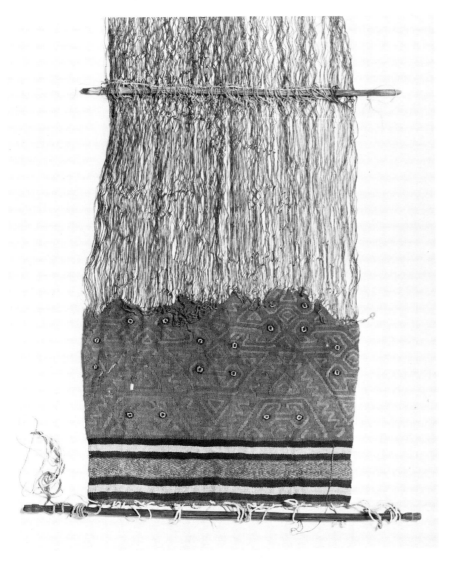

Photo 7. *Loom B (41.2/5483).* After restoration, showing working face of weaving—in position for weaver. *Courtesy of American Museum of Natural History.*

Notes on Restoration of the Looms
by Milica D. Skinner, February, 1966

Both looms lacked the heddle rods. Whoever removed them put cords in their place so the heddle lacings would remain in good order. The manner in which these were tied is indicated on the accompanying sketch (see Fig. 1). In order to properly repair the broken warps in their correct order these cords were untied, and modern heddle rods inserted to sustain the lacings. The cords were left in the lacings but cannot be retied without drawing the warps together.

Figure 1. *Original Heddle Lacing Ties.* These ties were used to keep heddle lacings in place. The knots, if properly set, would form the common granny. *Illustration by Nicholas Amorosi.*

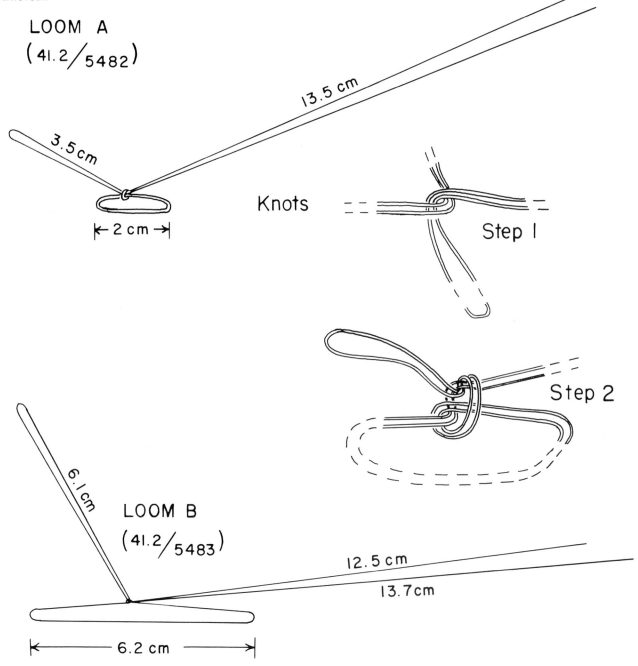

LOOM A
(41.2/5482)

13.5 cm

3.5 cm

2 cm

Knots

Step 1

Step 2

6.1 cm

LOOM B
(41.2/5483)

12.5 cm

13.7 cm

6.2 cm

The bobbins (?) used to replace the original loom bars were definitely put in place prior to burial. The substitution was casually done with no care taken that they pass through all the lashing cord loops and no attempt to secure properly the heading cords and to reset the lashings. The lashings of loom bar 2 on loom A were so irregularly pulled that this end selvedge could not be straightened without resetting some of the loops. Loops 6, 12 and 26 were hanging free and were not about the bobbin (?). Accordingly the bobbin (?)

was removed, the lashing cord loops readjusted to the points where the bends in them indicated the points where they crossed the heading, and they have been mounted in this position. From the size of these and the other loops it is evident that the original loom bars were about two centimeters in diameter.

If a substitute bar was used at the upper end of loom B, it was lost before we saw the specimen. About two-thirds of the white cotton weft at this end had disintegrated and the adjacent section of heading was missing. A "new" section of six-strand heading cord made of old white /\ cotton yarn (41.2/5162) was made, inserted in the warp end loops, and joined with adhesive to the original heading at the 82 and 83 warps, counted from the right selvedge. After warp breaks were repaired and tension equally distributed, this end was stitched to a strip of netting to hold all in order.

In loom A, 143 warps were found to be broken, of which 61 had two breaks, 21 had three breaks, two had four and one had five breaks. Seventeen were broken at the edge of the tapestry and had to have fine modern thread added so that they could be secured to the tapestry at the correct places. In 17 cases portions of warps were missing, so comparable Peruvian yarn of the same size, twist and color was added to each. In loom B, 63 warps were repaired; of these seven had two breaks and seven had three. None lacked sections, and only one had to be joined to the tapestry with modern thread.

Heddle lacings on each loom were of alternate type, that is, the lacing lapped over the sides of the heddle rod alternately (see Roth, 1950). Loom A lacing was unbroken up to the 225th warp, counting from the left. An old brown yarn was added to lift warps 225 and 227. On loom B, the lacing had five breaks between warps 2 and 4, 4 and 6, 20 and 22, 24 and 26, 26 and 30. Warp 28 has individual lifting loop. (Count made from right to left.)

Within the total warp counts the numbers of those warps added by the weaver are—loom A, counting left to right: numbers 69, 70; 103, 104; 136, 137; 166, 167; 179, 180; 193, 194. Loom B, counting right to left: 17, 18; 37, 38; 76, 77; 116, 117; 156, 157; 182, 183; 229. All of these added warps are slightly lighter in color and smaller in diameter than the balance of the warp.

During the warp repair of loom A, several errors made by the weaver were detected among the unbroken warps. Warp 7 is lifted by its original heddle lacing and is also caught by the loop lifting warp 9. In making the loop to lift the added warp, 137, it was also passed about warp 135, held by the original lacing. The following warps cross each other: 35 with 37, 36 with 38, 135 with 136, 166 with 167, 168. Number 222 in the tapestry crosses to become 223 at the other end, 223 becomes 224, 224 becomes 222. With continuation of weaving these crossings would have been left in the area of terminal weave.

In loom B there were no crossings noted, perhaps because more of these warps were found broken. Five warps had been broken and the breaks tied by the weaver.

In loom A at 44 cm. and at 64 cm. from loom bar were remnants of compounded cotton cords, similar to the lease cord of loom B. The few small residual pieces did not lie between the sheds but seemed to have encircled groups of warps in the manner of a running stitch. The numbers of warps so encircled could not be determined because of the breaks in the cord.

BIBLIOGRAPHY

Bird, Junius and Bellinger, Louisa. *Paracas Fabrics and Nazca Needlework.* Washington, D.C.: Textile Museum, 1954.

Roth, H. Ling. *Studies in Primitive Looms.* Halifax: Bankfield Museum. 3rd Edition, 1950, pp. 2-3.

Skinner, Milica D. "The Archaeological Looms from Peru in The American Museum of Natural History Collection". *Archaeological Textiles;* Irene Emery Roundtable on Museum Textiles, 1974 Proceedings. Washington, D.C.: Textile Museum. Patricia L. Fiske, ed. 1975.

SOME RUSH MATS WITH WARP MOVEMENT AS PATTERNING

BY NORA ROGERS

When one thinks of North American indigenous textiles, Navajo blankets or Chilkat twined capes come to mind. If you search a little further you may discover some very interesting textiles from the Great Lakes area. Probably the best known textiles of these Indian groups are the complex patterned storage bags and the plaited sashes. There is another textile of these groups that is worth knowing about—the rush mats, which have been shown very little attention by anthropologists and weavers alike.

My discovery of these exceptional mats occurred at the Denver Art Museum in April of 1981, while looking for spaced-weft twined mats and capes. The rush mats were rolled up and resting on dowels extending out from the wall—about three mats per pair of dowels. An outside mat caught my eye, for it had twining on the outer roll—an unexpected texture to see in woven rush mats. This happened to be the Menomini mat shown in Photo 1—a magnificent arrangement of color bands of twined patterns on each end juxtaposed with the real surprise, plain weave "op art" patterns in black and natural in the center panel. What a wonderful floor covering, sitting- or sleeping-mat! In the process of gathering photos of rush mats from other museums, I became aware of additional types of structures and designs in these rush mats. One that also interests me greatly is the diagonally plaited mat. (See Photo 2.)

In this article I will present the rush mats that have warp movement as the patterning device: those with twined, transposed warps and those that are diagonally plaited. Five were examined, mat in hand, in the Denver Art Museum. Several others were examined from photos provided by other museums and a few from published photos in literature. See page 20 for a list of museums that hold these types of mats in their collections.

These mats were made by the Woodland Lake groups who live in the areas near the Great Lakes, as well as those who lived there before being forced out into the eastern plains by European settlers. The groups are Menomini, Sauk and Fox, Winnebago, Potawatomi, Kickapoo and Ojibwa (also called Chippewa). Extant mats were woven during the 19th and early 20th centuries and they are no longer being woven. The knowledge very likely is now lost by the indigenous groups.

The twining structure of some of these mats has not been clearly nor completely recorded in the literature on rush mats. Petersen (1963) mentions the possibility of twining and gives a survey of the descriptions that imply twining: Kinietz and Jones (1942, p. 535); Densmore (1929, p. 156); and Lyford (1953, pp. 69, 90). However, Lyford's description is of weft twining and therefore must have been of the starting and finishing cords. Kinietz and Jones come closest to an accurate description of the structure of the warp twining; however, there are no diagrams.

The diagonally plaited structure is well documented in Shippen (1953), and Lyford (p. 90) describes it in one sentence. It is possible that Kinietz and Jones

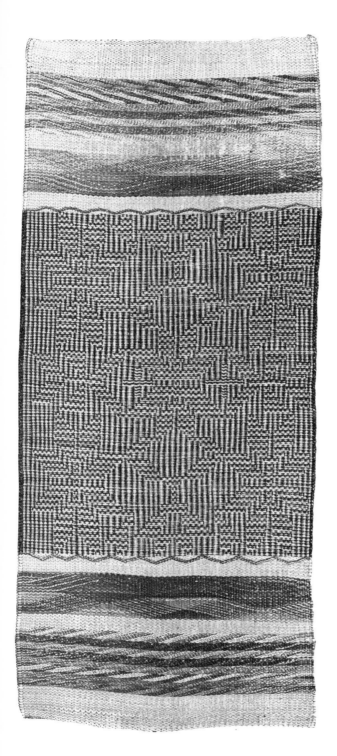

Photo 1. Menomini rush mat,
95″×43″. *Photo courtesy of Denver
Art Museum, Denver, Colorado.
Museum #1939.440.*

Photo 2. Kickapoo rush mat,
diagonally plaited structure. *Photo
courtesy of Denver Art Museum,
Denver, Colorado. Museum
#1939.428.*

(p. 535) are referring to it with the description ". . . by crossing the rushes over each other between the weft strands, which gives a zig zag appearance. . . . By this device rushes may be inclined diagonally across the mat. . . ."

A description of the process of weaving these mats by indigenous women might help understand the structure of the mats. An abridged, composite description follows. (Petersen (1963) gives a complete account of the gathering, preparation and dyeing of the rushes, the warp set-up, with diagrams, and the general weaving process of a Chippewa rush mat.)

The rushes are the warp elements and hang from a twined starting cord. The weft is plied nettle, Indian hemp, or basswood, and is much finer than the warp. The mats are almost warp face, with very little weft showing, and tend to be about 3½'×7', with the warp running the shorter distance. The width of the mat is determined by the length of the rushes.

For those of you who have learned the *ceinture fléchée* technique, creating the structure of these mats will feel familiar to your hands. There is no heddling device and no tensioning on the warps—in spite of the length of the mats (remember the weft runs the length of the mat). The shed is picked with the fingers, always working from left to right. The weft is discontinuous, being two-lengths-plus long and half-hitched two or three times in its middle to the left-hand edge cord. (See Fig. 1.) The upper half of the weft is taken across first—then the lower half, in the next shed, again from left to right. Another double-length-plus weft is then added, at its middle, to the left edge cord, and so on. Sometimes the end is just knotted to the right edge cord and then hangs out free. This can be seen in Photo 3. Other times the weaver threads the end back into the shed, or secures it to the edge cord with subsequent half-hitched wefts on the edge cord.

Both the starting and finishing edges are identical. The rush warps are twined together by the starting cord, which is the same fiber as the weft, usually. The warp ends are woven through each other and placed back through the starting cord, to form a beautiful basketry-type finish. (See Photo 3.) The twined starting cord is then lashed to a long pole that is tied to upright stakes, high enough that the rushes do not touch the ground. This starting cord is long enough to encompass all four sides of the mat. It serves as the starting cord in which the rush warps are twined; it then becomes doubled edge cords on each side to which the wefts are attached; and finally it becomes the finishing cord that twines across the bottom ends of the rush warps. (There are other versions of this, of course. Sometimes there are two or more joined cords traversing the four sides of the mat.) The edge cords are under tension during the weaving, being tied to the upright stakes several inches below the fell of the mat. The weaving progresses from top to bottom, the weft being pushed up into place. This is not an easy mode of weaving—the weft does not stay in place at all until it is forced into position by opening up the subsequent shed. Also, with no tension on the warps it is difficult to maintain an even weave or an even width. The latter is helped, however, by cords that are attached to the edge of the woven areas and tied to the side posts.

The weaver stands and works as rapidly as possible, with some pauses to moisten the rushes. If they dry out, the wefts do not pack up close enough together and the structure is weakened, or the rushes may become brittle and break. Work is started early in the morning when the air is damp and may be taken up again in the evening. In some cases a structure is built in which to weave the mat, and often a small one is built to store the materials when not in use. Lyford (1953) records that on a rainy day, with several women working, a mat may be woven in one day. Petersen (p. 246) recorded 27 hours for weaving and making the edges for a simple plain weave mat. I suspect the diagonally plaited mats and the complex patterned mats discussed here took much longer to complete.

With open-ended, free-hanging warps, possibilities of interesting structure and design occur. Both types of rush mats to be discussed exhibit an interdependence of design and structure that perhaps results from working with free-hanging warps as opposed to tensioned warps. A brief presentation of

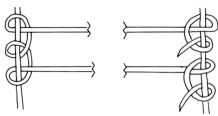

Figure 1. Course of a weft cord. Note that wefts in some mats are attached with a larkshead—only two loops around the left-hand edge cord. This causes the wefts to form a wedge from the edge into the woven area. Using three loops spaces the wefts apart a better distance, necessary for warp face weaving.

structure of the two types of mats follows, and later a discussion of design. Unfortunately, when writing, it is less confusing to present topics separately that would be truer to the textile if presented simultaneously.

Structure

The mats with twined patterning are basically plain weave, that is, interlacement of two perpendicular sets of elements—warp and weft. However, in the color bands of twined patterns on each end of the mat, the warps do move, one passive set through an adjacent active, twining set. There are many ways this is accomplished; the most common is shown in Figure 2. As I have found no description of this structure in the literature, it will be identified as twined, transposed warp movement. See Emery (1966, p. 188) for a description of transposed warp movement. The op art panels of the same mats (see Photos 1 and 4) are plain weave. To create the vertical lines, paired warps, one of each color, cross each other periodically to rearrange the color sequence. (See Fig. 3.)

Figure 2. Twined, transposed warp structure, expanded view. Detail is taken from color bands on far ends of the mat in Photo 1.

Figure 3. Structural diagram of center design panel from mat in Photo 1.

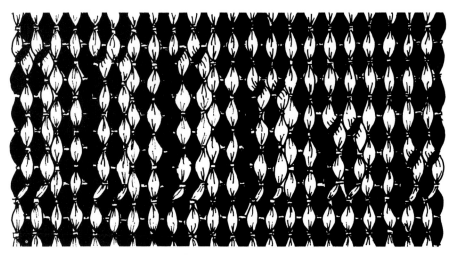

The diagonally plaited mats are actually three systems of elements, consisting of two diagonally moving systems (the warps) and a horizontal weft system. (See Fig. 4.) One can visualize this structure as diagonal plaiting with an added weft system. The weft system creates a good sturdy textile that won't pull on the bias as plaiting will do.

Figure 4. Structural diagram of diagonally plaited mats. Expanded view is shown to clarify movement of the two systems of warps.

A curious thing happens in the twined, transposed warp areas of the complex patterned mats: a slight ridge appears on one side of the mat, such as one might expect with twining juxtaposed against plain weave. But on the other side of the mat, no ridge occurs. The area has the look of plain weave! (If the Menomini mat at the Denver Art Museum had been rolled with the flat side showing, I might not be writing this article.) There is a clue, however, that what appears to be plain weave is actually twining. The diagonal color line(s) is continuous and well-defined, which is not possible in plain weave or diagonal plaiting. On looking closer, of course, one sees the paired warps twisting around each other as though being plied. The twining structure in Figure 2 can be compared with plain weave and diagonal plaiting in Figures 3 and 4. This difference from one side of the mat to the other side is shown in the following table.

Direction of Twine	Direction of Design Line	Twined Ridge?
S	\	yes
S	/	no
Z	\	no
Z	/	yes

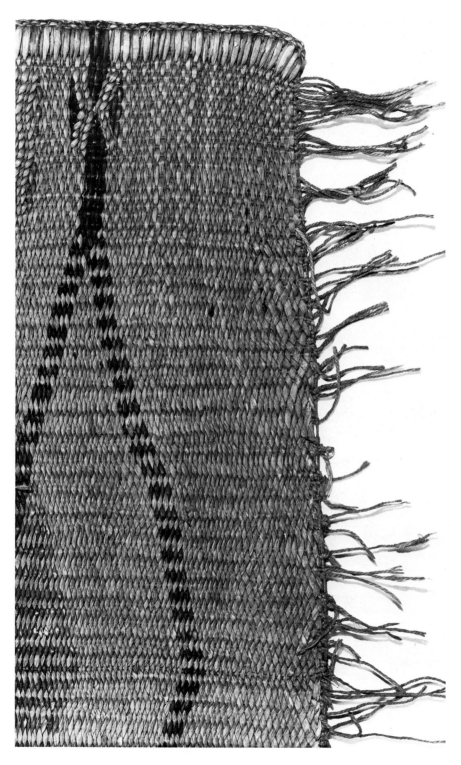

Photo 3. Detail of Kickapoo rush mat, showing woven basketry starting edge and free hanging weft cords knotted to selvedge cords. *Photo courtesy of Denver Art Museum, Denver, Colorado. Museum #1939.428.*

Photo 4. Detail of Photo 1 showing ridged diagonal pattern.

Photo 5. Opposite face of detail in Photo 4, showing flattening of twined areas.

Photo 6. Ridged side of diamond pattern, detail from Photo 1.

Photo 7. Opposite face of Photo 6, showing raised twined area with no ridges and valleys.

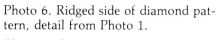

In most twined areas the first and second entries in the table hold. The third or fourth types occur infrequently in the mats examined. There is seemingly one consistency. The twine slope remains one direction in a given mat, with minor exceptions. So if the design line zigzags, the ridge comes and goes with the directional change of the line. And if pattern units are mirrored from one end of the mat to the other, as in Photo 1, one end has ridges and the other end does not. It is interesting that the effect is visual as well as dimensional. Not only does the ridge flatten out with the twine plying the opposite direction of the design line slope, but visually, in a drawing of the structure, the ridged effect dissipates. (See Fig. 5.)

A more striking example of this ridge vs. no ridge occurs in the diamond pattern areas of the Menomini mat shown in Photo 1. The warps which move diagonally through the twines take two weft rows to move from one twined pair to the next. On the ridged side of the mat, these moving warps travel over the weft when going through the twine and *under* the weft when "pausing" between the two diagonal twining pairs. This creates an even stronger indentation between the twined diagonal lines. On the reverse side the moving warps always travel *over* the weft between twined rows. Hence one has the impression of the whole area being the same structure—a slightly raised diamond area, consisting of contrasting diagonal lines. (See Photos 6 and 7, and Fig. 6.)

Design

DIAGONALLY PLAITED MATS. The diagonally plaited mats consist of at least two colors—natural and one dyed. As each color shows equally in this plaiting, a lovely diagonal plaid results from the movement of the colors through each other. Beginning with the warp arrangement at the starting cord, all odd numbered elements move one direction, while all even numbered elements move the opposite direction. (See Fig. 4.) The shapes that occur are geometric and consist of either solid color or horizontal lines of the two colors. Most of the diagonal plaited mats studied have natural rush as the background, i.e., the color that appears at the ends of the mats or the color that appears most frequently. Some mats include three or four colors, and in addition because the dye may be uneven, more than one shade of a color may appear. Even the natural rushes vary in shade intensity.

The arrangements of color are usually very carefully controlled and the widths of the stripes of color are consistent across the mat. Shippen (1953) records a mat that has 40 rushes for each color group. This exactness of count is not uncommon in the layout of the colors. Mirroring of color groups is frequent. Variation in color due to "dye lots" is often used in a controlled fashion to enhance the design. One example of a very pleasant variation that occurs within a color area follows: the warps are laid in the starting cord alternating dark and light, allowing diagonal lines within a moving color group. This happens in both the natural rush areas and the dyed color areas. This is a playfulness that makes these "plaid" mats even more interesting to the viewer.

The combinations of color are manifold: a unit of color can be simply one color. It can be bordered with a contrasting color. The color group can be very narrow—only two pairs wide. It can be several pairs wide. A multi-colored mat has constant interplay of color as the groups move diagonally through each other. One especially pleasing touch occurs in some mats by the addition of just one contrasting colored rush, seemingly randomly placed, amongst a wide band of solid color.

There is a reversal of plaiting direction in the vertical center of the mat and often at the quarter points. One Potawatomi mat shows five reversals, and a Sauk mat nine reversals. The width of the plaid, determined by how soon a reversal of plaiting direction occurs, can vary such that one color crosses many other colors. A color group can also remain contained in a narrow area by frequent reversals.

The shape of the diagonal "stitches", one row tilting to the left, the next to the right, gives added visual pleasure.

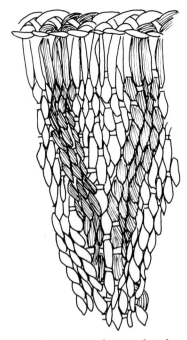

Figure 5. Drawing of arrowhead pattern from twined, transposed warp section of a rush mat. Note how prominent \ slope design line appears and how / slope disappears into plain weave.

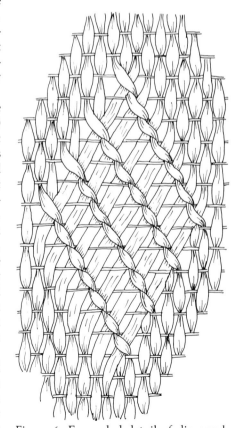

Figure 6. Expanded detail of diamond pattern from color bands near center panel of Photo 1. (Ridged side of design.)

COMPLEX PATTERNED MATS. The most complexly designed mats have a central panel of vertical line areas against a background of horizontal lines—an op art type of figure-ground design, which in weaving terminology is known as log cabin weave. The ends of the mats have vertical bands of color with twined diagonal designs, alternating with plain weave bands of natural rushes.

The center panel consists of either geometrical or figurative designs. The Menomini mat in Photo 1 has an arrangement of six-pointed geometrical shapes that seem related to some of the Ojibwa beadwork designs shown in Lyford (1953). Another one consists of rectangles within rectangles. Two Sauk and Fox mats have four underwater panthers in the center panel, one of these with another row of four-legged animals in profile. (See Photo 8.)

In log cabin weave, horizontal lines are created by alternating one light and one dark element. Vertical lines are created by pairing two light and two dark elements in sequence. But here the vertical lines are created by an eight- or twelve-unit arrangement of warp colors, so placed as to produce "spots" on each side of the vertical lines. (See Fig. 7.) The open-ended warps allow rearrangement of colors so that the weaver can place vertical-line patterns pretty much wherever she wishes against the horizontal-line background. However, some considerations have to be made. Shapes that include a diagonal edge must be placed such that the vertical-line figures will be well defined and not blend into the background at the figure's edge. The angle and size of a diagonal shape is limited by this feature. Some very narrow vertical-line pattern areas present a different problem of not having enough warp ends to use the eight-or twelve-unit color arrangement. This is solved by sequencing two light and two dark elements as commonly found in log cabin weave color arrangements.

The bands of color bordering the center panel to the edge of the mat are the locations of the twined, transposed warp patterns. Twining allows well-defined, continuous diagonal lines, the basic design lines in all the color bands in these complex patterned mats. The designs can best be described as parallel diagonal lines forming arrow shapes, diamonds, zigzags or waves, and diagonal bands. The texture and light-reflecting qualities inherent in the twining juxtaposed against the plain weave are important facets of the design.

I found many other mats with the same designs as the complex patterned mats, but with a different layout. These have no center panel, but one or more bands of colored designs repeating in some orderly sequence across the length of the mat. The designs in the bands are the twined diagonals *plus* the geometric log cabin type. Here the log cabin designs, which are so elaborate in the center panels of the complex patterned mats, are simplified and narrow. (Vertical lines are created by two dark and two light color sequences rather than the eight- or twelve-unit color arrangements.) There are no figurative designs, only geometric ones. Usually the twined, transposed warp patterns in these color bands are similar to the ones in the complex patterned mats. In some cases, however, the twined warp movement becomes much freer, creating linear designs. The colored rushes almost become embroidery, giving the illusion of being added to the pre-woven mat, appearing and disappearing, seemingly moving at angles determined by the weaver and not by the structure of the mat.

Of course there are many combinations of design that don't fit so nicely into these categories: a Chippewa plain weave mat that has a large central panel of geometric log cabin design with just plain weave bands of color as border; a Menomini mat that has three rather wide bands with blocks of log cabin weave, with bands of colored plain weave interspersed; a very special Kickapoo diagonally plaited mat that shows a small twined pattern between the color bands at the starting and finishing ends of the mat (Photo 2); a Winnebago mat with four horizontal bands of warp floats across the length of the mat travelling across six vertical bands of log cabin weave which employ both the two light and two dark color sequences *and* the eight-unit color arrangements! The combinations and variations of these design units and their

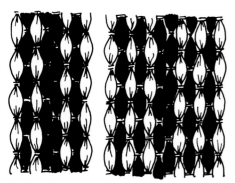

Figure 7. Arrangement of warp colors for vertical line shapes in "op art" designs.

Photo 8. Fox mat of complex patterning. *Photo courtesy of Denver Art Museum, Denver, Colorado. Museum #1971.589.*

layout across the mat must be endless and as numerous as there are weavers and mats. While categories help discussion of design, they often fall short of a good description of what actually occurs over the multitude of rush mats that have been woven.

Color combinations most frequently found in the mats studied are purple, magenta and green with natural, sometimes with black in the center panel. Other combinations are: dark blue, red, purple with natural; green and natural; red orange, green and black; mauve and pale green (both faded?) with natural; yellow, black and natural; red, green, maroon and natural; purple, brown and natural; black, brown and natural; black, brown, green and natural; green, red and natural; black, green, maroon, ochre and natural; and maroon, ochre and natural.

Design and Structure

With the exception of the op art center panels, design and structure in these mats are interdependent. In the diagonally plaited mats the diagonal movement of the warps through each other sets up an interplay of the colors that is unique to this structure. Both systems show as they move through each other. It is not at all like a plain weave plaid turned on its diagonal side. The two systems are not perpendicular to each other, but meet at a much lesser angle, closer to 45°. Hence the visible amount of color and the angle of the color lines are determined by the structure. The weaver determines the colors and the width of the color groups when laying the warps into the starting cord. This cannot be altered during weaving. She can choose the number and placement of directional reversals of the warp movement as she weaves. The combination of her choices and the structure determine the overall visual effect.

In the mats with twined, transposed warp movement, there is diagonal movement of warps in these pattern bands and this diagonal movement creates the shapes and lines of the patterns. Here the warps move through each other as in the diagonally plaited mats. But one very significant structural change completely alters the visual effect: one set of warps twines in pairs while the other set moves passively through the active, twining pairs and is hidden from view during this movement. The twined warps appear on both sides of the mat and create solid blocks of lines of color as they move diagonally for a given number of weft throws. (For example, three pairs of warps will move for six weft throws, creating a parallelogram.) By controlling which colored warps are the active twining warps and which are the passive warps, the weaver creates her pattern shapes—parallel wedges, arrowheads, diamonds, waves, etc.; or perhaps "otter tails", by combining the diagonal shapes themselves in different sequences; perhaps combining the shapes with non-moving colored warps; or with the same moving warps idling in plain weave for a few shots of weft; or with different numbers of moving warps. Innumerable pattern shapes are created by various combinations of plain weave and the continuous diagonal lines—all controlled by structural manipulation. Color choices provide another dimension to the already existing structurally controlled aspects. In these mats the inventiveness of the weaver is truly displayed, much as a virtuoso performance of an opera diva showing off her vocal abilities in the cadenza. Each mat is a unique version of these assemblages of color and structural choices.

Structurally Related Textiles

While the structures of these mats are unusual, perhaps even unique, there are a few textiles that appear related. The three system structure has a cousin in basketry—hexagonal plaiting, where all three systems are of equal size, tend to be rigid, and do move through each other in the same manner as the elements in the diagonal plaited rush mats. The fact that the rush mats have two elements identical (warps) and one much finer (weft) creates a completely different effect—the warp face quality with tilted rows, first one direction, then the other. While the two structures are almost identical, the effect is quite different.

A more distant cousin of the three system structure is found in the spaced-weft twined storage bags of the Woodland Indians. Some of these bast fiber bags, the ones used for corn hulling (see Whiteford, 1977, p. 54), have the warps travelling diagonally, one set each direction, but with the warps remaining in their own planes. They do *not* interlace. Rather, the twined wefts hold the systems of warps in position as they cross each other. The appearance is of long diagonal lines travelling one direction on the face of the textile crossed by ribs of the weft twining. The viewer can just see the diagonal lines travelling the other direction on the reverse side through the front plane.

Anne Blinks has replicated a textile which is related to the twined, transposed warp structure — a twined bag, possibly made by Delaware Indians during the 17th century, and presented by Ulla Cyrus-Zetterstrom (1978). This bag consists structurally of alternating vertical panels of spaced-weft twining and warp-face twined plaiting. It is the twined plaited bands that interest us. The structure of the bands is a true form of plaiting; that is, the warp element, in this case from the right-hand edge, interlaces (as though weft) through the complete set of warps, arriving at the left-hand edge to become a warp element again with the subsequent shed. The unusual aspect is that the warps are twined in pairs, and the outer single warp acts as weft, rather than both warps that make up the twining pair. (This bag seems particularly important for ethnographic textile study for two reasons: First, warp twining is not a common structure in textiles in North America. Second, the weaver employed two types of warp patterned structure in one textile: 1) the spaced-weft twining, as found in storage bags of the Woodland Lake Indians, and 2) the twined plaiting which is not found in other textiles in this geographical area, but is definitely related to the warp face diagonally plaited structure of the sashes (*ceinture fléchée*) of the Woodland and Northeast Indian groups.)

The commonality of the two structures — twined, transposed warps of the mats and twined plaiting of the bags — lies in the diagonal warp movement, the twining of warps, *and* the inclusion of a separate weft. Contrasts are: 1) all warps are twined in the bag (except when acting as weft), while in the mats, only those warps that are the active, moving elements are twined. The warps twine or weave, depending on their role at a given point. 2) The movement of the passive warps through the active twining warps begins at different positions in the pattern band. This can best be shown in Figure 8. As you can see, in the plaiting, the passive movement begins at the outside edge of the band; in the transposed warp structure, the passive movement begins at the center of the pattern, immediately adjacent to the edge of the twining warps.

Figure 8. Structural comparison of twined, transposed warp movement (left) and twined plaiting (right).

It does seem appropriate to emphasize the relationship of the plain weave transposed warp structure with the *twined*, transposed warp structure. The latter could be considered an embellishment of the plain weave structure — though the extant examples of the two structures are geographically separated by thousands of miles. The plain weave structure is found in Argentina, Peru and Chile. (See Emery, p. 188 and Rowe, p. 104.) These are warp-face textiles and the structure seems to have the same design intent as the twined weave — continuous diagonal lines or bands, combined with vertical movement. It is interesting to note that the plain weave movement was woven most likely on back strap looms with the warp under tension, while the Woodland Lake twined version was accomplished with free-hanging warps. It would be good to find out if the free-hanging warps encourage twining and if the tensioned warps discourage twining.

In summary, we have looked at some rush mats, woven in the 19th and early 20th centuries by Woodland Lake Indian groups, with two unusual structures: 1) diagonal plaiting with weft (three systems of elements) and 2) plain weave with isolated areas of twined, transposed warps. We have noted an interdependence between design and structure and a comprehensive and imaginative use of these facets by the weavers. In addition we have briefly glanced at some structurally related textiles.

This study has been extremely rewarding for me. It has illuminated yet another fascinating textile of these Woodland Lake Indian groups, adding it to my awareness of their inventiveness and skills in the weaving tradition. Realizing the beauty and complexity of the rush mats *and* the storage bags and plaited sashes, my strong query is, what were the ancestors of these textiles? What a tremendous loss that we have no remains of the antecedents! Since the first Europeans did not trade for these textile goods as the explorers did for the Northwest Indian textiles, and since archaeological finds in this geographical area turn up very few and minor textiles plus pottery sherds with textile imprints, the likelihood of uncovering this knowledge is miniscule. Perhaps we shall have to be satisfied with only the recent creations of these people as being a rich culmination of their textile heritage. How unfortunate the skills are lost to their people. It is a loss to all cultures, as these textiles could have developed even further, beyond anything we know of at this time.

Museums that hold rush mats in their collections:
  Chandler Institute, Mission, South Dakota
  Denver Art Museum, Denver, Colorado
  Field Museum of Natural History, Chicago, Illinois
  Milwaukee Public Museum, Milwaukee, Wisconsin
  Museum of the American Indian, Heye Foundation, New York
  National Museum of Natural History (Smithsonian), Washington, D.C.
  Peabody Museum of Archaeology and Ethnology, Cambridge,
    Massachusetts
  Washington State Museum, Seattle, Washington

This is a partial list, as not all museums responded to queries.

BIBLIOGRAPHY

Cyrus-Zetterstrom, Ulla. "A North American Indian Bag in Twining Technique", *Journal of the Royal Armoury*. Stockholm. vol. XIV:12, 1978.

Densmore, Frances. "Chippewa Customs", *Bureau of American Ethnology, Bulletin* 86. 1929.

Emery, Irene. *The Primary Structures of Fabrics*. Washington, D.C.: Textile Museum, 1966.

Kinietz, W. Vernon and Volney H. Jones. "Notes on the Manufacture of Rush Mats Among the Chippewa", *Michigan Academy of Science, Arts and Letters, Papers*, vol. 27, 1942, pp. 525-538.

Lyford, Carrie. *Ojibwa Crafts*. Lawrence, Kansas: Bureau of Indian Affairs, 1953.

Petersen, Karen Daniels. "Chippewa Mat-weaving Techniques". *Bureau of American Ethnology, Bulletin* 186, 1963, pp. 211-286.

Rowe, Ann Pollard. *Warp-Patterned Weaves of the Andes*. Washington, D.C.: Textile Museum, 1977.

Shippen, H.H. "A Woven Bulrush Mat from an Indian Tribe of the Great Lakes Region". *Michigan Academy of Science, Arts and Letters, Papers*, vol. 39, 1954, pp. 399-406.

Whiteford, Andrew Hunter. "Fiber Bags of the Great Lakes Indians". *American Indian Art Magazine*, vol. 2, no. 3. Summer, 1977, pp. 52-64, 85.

A more complete bibliography on Chippewa rush mats is given in Karen Daniels Petersen's article listed above.

FAUGUSTINO'S FAMILY
Knitters, Weavers and Spinners on the Island of Taquile, Peru

BY MARY FRAME

The island of Taquile sits stonily near the western shore of Lake Titicaca, the highest navigable lake in the world, cupped in the *altiplano* of the Andes. This island is all inclines and the surface is corrugated with stone walls which terrace the hillsides and define small, irregular plots of cultivated land. Camouflaged paths of bedrock and laid stones crisscross the island and the houses, made of field stone, meld into the landscape. No cars, no sounds of motors intrude. There is a harmony of humanscape and landscape, the one edging into the other.

I drew up on the island of Taquile in a boat operated by island men. In the three hour trip from the lakeshore town of Puno, I had chatted with the few day-trip tourists who shared the launch, while concentrating on the handmade clothes of the boat operators: a white, coarsely woven wool shirt with full sleeves attached to a dropped shoulder line, black or navy full-length trousers and a sleeveless white vest with black front and side panels. To this basic costume, each man added some finely worked fabrics in dark red or maroon. Several wore wide, cummerbund-like belts with horizontal bands of white figurative designs. Another wore, tied at his waist, a flat, squarish bag with two tiny pockets. They all wore large, knitted caps. The caps sat high on their heads, with the tasselled end hanging forward at one side of the jaw.

Among the passengers on the boat, there was one miniature version of the Taquile boatmen, an 11 year old named Faugustino Quispe Grus. After sitting together a while and sharing my breakfast pastries, I asked Faugustino about his knitted cap, which was maroon and patterned only halfway up, the rest being pure white. He told me he had knitted it himself, in the style of the *soltero*, or unmarried man. After he married, he could wear the completely patterned maroon hat, like the older boat operators. This was not the first hat he had knitted but the seventh or eighth. He had begun knitting when he was eight and, like virtually all Taquile males, he had become proficient in handling the fine threads and creating the distinctive patterns. He asked me if I wanted to buy his hat and we quickly closed the deal: I was delighted to have the hat, crafted by an 11 year old in a quality I could not match, and he was pleased with the money. Though he was bareheaded for the next hour, he knew his other caps awaited him at home. We talked about the designs he had worked on his *chullu*, or cap—the ducks, the doves, the X-shaped crossroad, the S-shaped port and the six-part circle that symbolizes the six crops raised on the island of Taquile (Photo 1). He had forgotten the meaning of some of the designs but he assured me his father, Augustin, and his brother-in-law, Gonzalo, knew all of those things, and, furthermore, that they both wove bayeta, the rough fabric used to make the shirts, vests and trousers worn by Faugustino and the boat operators. I asked if he would take me to meet his father on the following day and he agreed as the boat pulled up at the first landing stage on the far side of Taquile. Here, below the village, the day-trip

Photo 1. Three styles of Taquile knitted caps. Faugustino's cap is on the right.

visitors alighted. In two hours, they would be picked up on the other side of the island.

At the second landing stage, I set foot on Taquile and was met by a man, also dressed like the boat operators, with a notebook in his hand. I was quickly handed on to a shyly smiling woman in a bright pink sweater, full-gathered black skirt and a long black headcloth with brilliant corner tassels. She immediately shouldered my backpack and set off, up the stony path, but not before Faugustino told me that this was his married sister, Pelagia, with whom I would be staying. By the chance rotation of housing visitors with island families, I was to stay with Faugustino's family.

I plodded behind Pelagia, packless but still labouring in the thin air, my eyes fixed on the bright hem cording of her several skirts and her brown legs and bare feet. She moved fluidly up the stone steps of the path, seeming not to notice the weight of my pack, the incline or the irregular stones that tripped me up. And then, we were on the level in a courtyard, amid puddles of drying vegetables, clay water jugs and, in one corner, the skeletal framework of a loom. Stone cottages edged the courtyard on three sides and, beyond a wall, was a view over the southern slopes of Taquile to the lake, with its reflections of blue sky and the heaped-up clouds that obscured the horizon. Two steps led up to the packed earth floor of my cottage which was crowded with sacks of vegetables, piles of cloth, a table and a stone sleeping platform which was made inviting by reed wall mats and a generous supply of wool blankets. I added my down sleeping bag and stretched out in my cozy nest to orient myself to my new surroundings. Flecks of blue sky pricked through the twig thatch of the roof. My eyes roamed over the orderly lashing of poles that supported the pitched roof and came to rest on a series of spindles tucked into the roof, each with a neat cone of fine, black yarn. In one corner, a cascade of white yarns trailed from two loom harnesses suspended from a pole which rested on the thick walls. Several knitted caps and an assortment of folded ponchos, shawls, vests and belts topped large sacks of vegetables. Contentedly, I relaxed, knowing I would have many opportunities to observe the processes of fabric-making within the family.

As news of my arrival spread to the family, I began to receive visitors. Marcialina, the six year old sister of Faugustino and Pelagia, popped in to try out my felt pens. Their father, Augustin Quispe Mamani, and Pelagia's husband, Gonzalo Yucra Huatta, next came to greet me. Both Augustin and Gonzalo spoke Spanish as they, like Faugustino, had attended the island school and they were the ones who would answer my questions in the coming days. Pelagia and her mother, Candelaria Grus Machegua, appeared and, with smiles, they made me welcome. They both spoke Quechua, the indigenous language of Taquile and many other parts of Peru, which I do not understand. However, learning about textiles in Peru is not necessarily a verbal activity and I, like the young Taquile girls, learned from Pelagia and Candelaria by watching. One more small person named Elias, who was the son of Gonzalo and Pelagia, made his appearance later in the day, swaddled in white cloths and bound firmly with a wide belt of his mother's. Other relatives living nearby would appear later.

In the following days, I looked at the family's fabrics, watched them spin, weave and knit clothes for themselves and for each other, as well as ones they were willing to sell to me for a museum in Canada. They embraced my project of collecting everyday wear for a man and a woman as well as technological examples of the fabric making processes. From their own surplus of garments, they offered certain items. What they couldn't supply me with almost surely appeared in the hands of a member of their extended family. They finished incomplete garments and started new ones so that I would have photographs and examples of the processes as well as the finished garments. And, with their cooperation, I was able to ask straightforward questions on delicate topics, like the men's under-trousers.

All of this was done at intervals during the day, particularly in the late afternoon and even by lamplight. Besides farming and tending their sheep, the family's major activity was the carpentry for the interior of the adjacent Adventista Church. Every day except Saturday, the congregation appeared for work. Pelagia and Candelaria cooked the mid-day meal for as many as 50 people. This project was the reason Pelagia and Gonzalo were staying in her parents' house, instead of their own house near the south end of the island. While they worked, I had time to walk the island paths, write notes and buy some items from the array of handmade fabrics for sale to visitors in the cooperative store in the village.

I was able to see that the uniform of the Taquile boatmen that I had first observed was generally typical of the way men and boys dressed on a daily basis. Likewise, Pelagia's layered skirts, headcloth and bright sweater were typical of women's wear. What I didn't notice at first was the differences in designs and stripe arrangements in the red patterned fabrics, like belts and bags. I cannot "read" the patterned fabrics, but it is clear to me, from the explanations of particular fabrics, that the people of Taquile can. The choice of designs can indicate an article was woven for a particular fiesta or a life cycle event, like marriage. A wedding *chuspa*, or coca leaf bag, woven for the marriage of Augustin's eldest son, Rosento, by his wife, Dionysia, had a motif of a spiked diamond with triangles on the ends of the spikes. Augustin said this symbol represented a particular dance performed at weddings. The same motif appeared on the wide belt Gonzalo was wearing. His belt had been woven for the occasion of a friend's wedding in which he had participated. Some of the patterned fabrics made for special events, like Gonzalo's belt, come to be worn on a daily basis; others are carefully stored, to be worn only at particular times. Sometimes, hats, vests and belts are worn inside out, keeping the right side clean for something more than daily wear. But Gonzalo explained a further reason for wearing his wide red belt inside out. Among the designs was a bird in flight, flying to the left. When worn right side out, with white designs on a red background, the direction the bird flies is an auspicious symbol. Wearing the belt inside out, with the bird flying to the right, can indicate that something is wrong, like a death in the family. Each warp-patterned fabric has a large number of designs, some of a generally propitious nature that occur on many pieces and others that are quite specific to an occasion. The stripes of contrasting color that border the pattern bands can carry other information, like the individual status of the wearer (Zorn, 1979, p. 214). The subtleties of language are encoded in the warp-patterned fabrics they make and wear and the people of Taquile share an easy fluency in this visual language.

On a more general and comprehensible level, it was possible for me to see that several fabric traditions mix in the costumes worn on Taquile. The fine red fabrics with the visual language of warp-patterned designs continue an indigenous tradition that stretches back through pre-Columbian times. Rectangular fabrics with four selvedges are woven on staked-out ground looms and they are constructed into mantas, coca leaf bags, belts, etc., by no more than sewing edges. In the indigenous tradition, the fabric is not cut but merely assembled or used in the shape it had on the loom. The fabric itself has closely spaced warps and the patterns are picked up by hand in complementary and float weave structures. The form of some of the fabrics, like the distinctive coca leaf bag with exterior pockets, has a history that goes back at least to A.D. 700.

The conquest of Peru by the Spanish in the 1530's brought radical changes in all things, including clothing. They introduced tailored clothing and the novelty of cutting woven fabric to correspond to the body's contours before sewing it together. They also introduced the harness loom with treadles for weaving bayeta fabric, a plain or twill woven fabric from which the tailored shirts, vests, trousers and skirts are cut. Sheep were introduced by the Spanish and provided a warm alternative to the indigenous alpaca for the loosely woven bayeta. Knitting with two or more needles was also a post-conquest introduction. Later changes to the Taquile fabric tradition come from continuing contact with industrialization. Factory made blankets and sweaters, truck tire sandals, dress shirts and buckle belts are used on Taquile, along with

Photo 2. A treadle loom with a
bayeta warp incompletely mounted.

Photo 3. Augustin attaching woven
bayeta to the cloth beam of a treadle
loom.

Photo 4. Faugustino winding bobbins
for bayeta weaving.

Photo 5. Augustin weaving bayeta.

aniline dyes, synthetic yarns and treadle sewing machines.

In Faugustino's family, the division of textile tasks reflects the mixture of traditions present in their costumes. Augustin and Gonzalo weave bayeta on the treadle loom and cut and sew the Spanish-derived tailored clothes for the family. They, and 11 year old Faugustino, knit as well. On the other hand, Pelagia and Candelaria weave warp-faced fabrics on staked-out ground looms. The perpetuation of the indigenous fabric tradition appears to rest solely with the women while the men employ the imported technology to make clothes in the Spanish-influended style. Yarn spinning tasks are shared, but in general the finest spinning is done by the women while the men help with the coarser spinning.

Bayeta Weaving

The bulk of the fabric for the family's basic clothes is bayeta and it is woven on a two- or four-harness, counter-balanced loom with treadles (Photo 2). The skeleton of the loom sits permanently in the courtyard and the partially woven warp is stored in the house between weaving sessions. The warp remains threaded through the harnesses and beater and the entire assembly, with pulleys suspended from a cross-bar and treadles dangling from the harnesses, is moved indoors. The family possesses several sets of loom "innards" that can be mounted on the same rustic framework in the courtyard, allowing them to work alternately on several types of bayeta. A drawback to this rational use of equipment was betrayed when Augustin discovered a rat had chewed through bunches of warp while it was stored in the house. Much laborious warp mending ensued before he could begin weaving. As a weaver, I was most impressed with Augustin's equanimity in the face of the damaged warp.

The length of bayeta that Augustin was working on was a two-harness, balanced plain weave fabric of white synthetic yarns. After suspending the shedding assembly by positioning the cross-bar on top of the framework and attaching the cloth beam, he and Gonzalo straightened the warp. The warp chain was partially undone, stretched across the courtyard and anchored around a large rock. Augustin attached the end of the woven fabric by passing it between two small slats which fit into the grooved roller of the cloth beam (Photo 3). The slats were slipped back under ties which held them firmly in their groove and the cloth was securely pinched between the slats. He then wound on most of the woven cloth and fixed a simple tenterhook, with a nail point at each end, across the fabric near the fell. While Augustin and Gonzalo mended the rat-chewed warp, Faugustino wound bobbins, a job he was apparently quite used to (Photo 4). He arranged a loop from the roof of one of the cottages and the two yarns were delivered to him through the loop at an even tension. The bobbins were wound neatly with a built-up node of yarn at each end. With warps mended and bobbins wound, Augustin set to weaving, his bare feet almost wrapping around the treadles. He threw the boat shuttle, changed the shed and swung the overhead beater, knocking the wefts into the growing fabric (Photo 5).

In bayeta weaving, threads and threadings are chosen for specific uses. Under-trousers, shirts and vests are frequently made from sheep's wool, single-ply yarns in a plain, balanced weave on two harnesses. Commercial, synthetic yarns are also used for the same garments. The synthetic yarns are valued for their pristine whiteness and long-wearing qualities, but the warmth of sheep's wool is appreciated in the cold weather of July and August. Trouser fabric is often twill woven on four harnesses at a closer sett and in dark colored synthetic or handspun yarns. Skirting can be plain or twill woven in handspun wool or brilliant synthetic yarns of pink, scarlet, orange, yellow, green or royal blue. Lighter weights of handspun wool appear in the women's head-cloth, or *chucu*, and in their blouses, now largely replaced in daily wear by bright pullover sweaters. Candelaria's wool blouse, which was sold to me for the museum, was dyed a deep red after it was sewn together.

A distinctive man's garment, not described so far, is woven on the treadle

Photo 6. Augustin posing as Officer of the Port — wearing *chal.*

Photo 7. Augustin knitting a *chullu,* or cap.

Photo 8. Detail of a knitted front panel of a fiesta vest, or *chaleco musico,* showing men and women dancing among other designs typical of Taquile knitted fabrics.

loom. The *chal*, or long scarf, is usually a gleaming white, twill-woven fabric with a largle-scale blue check. It is finely woven and has a band of prismatic colors a short distance from either end. Today, the band of rainbow colors is generally put into the weft, but some older examples have colorful crocheted discs as well. Synthetic yarns have largely replaced sheep's wool yarns in contemporary examples. The *chal* is usually folded once along each axis and worn hanging over one shoulder or over both shoulders (Photo 6). In everyday wear, it is often wrapped around the waist, over top of the wide red belt.

Some bayeta garments are rarely seen on a day-to-day basis. Black waist-length jackets with stand-up collars were worn by all the male community officials at a fiesta I attended. Augustin had a black jacket and said he was entitled to wear it as this year's 'Officer of the Port'. Candelaria also had a black jacket she had worn when she married Augustin. Large amounts of bayeta are obviously required by the family for daily wear and special occasions, and it is accepted that Augustin and Gonzalo will produce the fabric and make the clothes for themselves, their wives and unmarried children.

Knitting

Knitting is also man's work. With a ball of yarn stuffed in each trouser pocket and the two yarns passing around his neck from opposite sides to his knitting, Augustin walked or sat, chatting, without missing a stitch (Photo 7). He was knitting a man's cap, or *chullu*, in spiralling rows on five metal needles. Augustin bought double-ended knitting needles in Puno and fashioned a flattened hook on one end of each needle. The hooked end appeared to help him feel the stitches without looking at them. The stitches were divided approximately evenly on four needles, and the fifth needle was used to transfer the stitches as they were knitted from one of the other needles. He used no more than two major colors at one time, usually white and maroon or white and navy, and those were the two colors he held in his pockets. In the two-color design bands, the color that he was not knitting with was carried along on the inside of the knitting and caught into the structure every few stitches to prevent long floats. Four or five other colors were introduced for small motifs. These extra colors were used for a few stitches, then left hanging on the inside where they were picked up on the subsequent turn of the spiral row to be used for another few stitches. Augustin was using a maroon commercial yarn he had dyed and a two-ply, handspun white wool.

The patterns on his *chullu* included several types of birds, a butterfly and geometric patterns representing roads, crossroads and the six crops of Taquile. By knitting in odd moments of the day, Augustin and Gonzalo could knit a cap in a week. Faugustino said it took him about a month to make one, but then a young boy has many more distractions.

Besides the married and unmarried styles of *chullus*, or caps, already mentioned, there is another style worn by toddlers. It has a frill-like brim along the lower edge, except for a small gap placed at the back of the neck. The one I bought from Gonzalo's brother-in-law had the name of his child, Selvano, knitted into it. Selvano was immediately promoted to wearing the *soltero*, or unmarried, style of hat. Gonzalo's baby son, Elias, sported still another style of *chullu*. His was a shorter cap with ear flaps, worked in white sheep's wool with geometric patterns in natural shades of alpaca yarn. In theory, the form of the *chullu* can indicate status but, in practice, Augustin and Gonzalo frequently wore the half-patterned version of the unmarried man, possible leftovers from their single days.

Knitting is used for decorating quite a different garment. The front panels of the *chaleco musico*, a bayeta vest worn for some fiestas, are knitted in the same stye as the caps. Most vests have a row of men and women, hands joined in dance, across the chest area (Photo 8), as well as alpacas, butterflies, flowers and geometric patterns. One of the masked characters in the Fiesta of San Isidro dramatics wore a *chaleco musico*, but otherwise, I did not see the vest being worn.

Fibers and Yarns

Spinning and twisting yarns is a constant employment shared by the family. On the paths or among the visiting relatives in Augustin's house, the women were most consistently at the spinning tasks. However, both men and women spun sheep's wool on the drop spindle for the coarser fabrics (Photo 9). Gonzalo said that the women, like his wife Pelagia, were better able to make the fine-spun yarns that would later be plied for knitting or warp-patterned weaving. When spinning fine yarns, Pelagia supported the tip of the spindle on the ground (Photo 10). In this way, the heavy spindle did not endanger the delicate yarn. Pelagia differentiated fine weaving and knitting yarns by the amount of twist she put in at the spinning and plying stages. Extra twist is used to make the warp-faced weaving yarns stronger and less hairy. Moderate twist in spinning and plying keeps the knitting yarns softer and more suited to the flexible, looped structure.

Today, many commercially-spun synthetic and wool yarns of various sizes are used in the fabrics of Taquile. The increasing use of these yarns does not appear to be simply tied to saving time, although that may be a factor. Faugustino's family has only five sheep and, according to Gonzalo, fleece is not always easy to buy. Furthermore, a vest woven of synthetic yarns will last for five years in daily use, as opposed to three years for one made of handspun wool yarns. When commercial yarns are used, they are sometimes reprocessed to produce the yarn characteristics suitable for the finished fabric. For example, commercial yarns that will be used in warp-faced fabrics are over-twisted on the drop spindle to produce the hard-twist favored for these firm fabrics. In the finished article, it is often difficult to tell handspun yarns from overtwisted commercial yarns, and in fact, they are freely combined. Commercial yarns are used without further processing for bayeta weaving and knitting. The family's knowledge of yarns is unquestionable, but they are pragmatic about yarn choice. They consider what is available at what price, what wears well and what appeals to their eye. In many cases, their choice is a clear-hued synthetic yarn. The astute Augustin read, in my questions, my own prejudice for handspun yarns and pragmatically offered to make more articles using handspun yarn, if I was returning next year.

Alpaca is the traditional fiber in the *altiplano* of southern Peru and has been since ancient times. The family does not own any alpacas, and because alpaca is a valued export, it is more difficult and expensive to buy. However, one elegant garment for men and one for women continue to be made of alpaca, at least partially. The man's poncho is pure black, relieved by four or six fine red lines. The woman's carrying cloth is similarly colored but smaller in size and without the neck slit. The handspun warp is made of one strand of black sheep's wool and one strand of black alpaca which are plied together very firmly in preparation for warp-faced weaving. The weft is sheep's wool, but it is hidden entirely by the closely spaced warps. Although the garments are less than one-half alpaca, the luster and smoothness of the alpaca dominates the finished fabric. Older decorated fabrics from Taquile were often made of pure alpaca, but the family used the fine grades of alpaca sparingly, restricting it to the black garments and a few knitted design bands. They used coarser grades of alpaca, or perhaps llama fiber, in sacks, ropes and smaller carrying cloths.

Warp-Patterned Weaving

The most traditional fabrics, which are warp-faced and frequently warp-patterned, are woven by the women. Like the fabrics of ancient times, the warp is continuous and the shedding devices are applied to the stretched warp. A shed rod and looped heddles are used to open the shed for weft insertion. Unlike the loom used for bayeta, where the warp loops are cut and threaded through the harnesses and reed, the warp loops at both ends are maintained and the entire warp is woven, producing a fabric with four selvedges. The loom is very portable as it is no more than the threads themselves, the cross-bars they are mounted on, the applied shedding devices and four ground

Photo 9. Gonzalo spinning sheep's wool for bayeta on a drop spindle.

Photo 10. Pelagia holding Elias and spinning fine yarn with the spindle tip supported on the ground.

stakes to which the cross-bars are lashed.

Warping and weaving are done close to the ground with the warps stretched horizontally. Candelaria and Pelagia warped together, passing the yarns back and forth in a figure eight between shed sticks, tensioning and laying them in closely packed order as they went (Photo 12). They were warping a belt of moderate width with three pattern bands, such as an adolescent boy like Faugustino might wear. When Pelagia departed to get the evening meal ready, Augustin took over for her and passed the yarn back to Candelaria who was dictating the color order at her end. After the warping was done, Candelaria worked on her own, tying loop heddles to the warp, transferring the warp loops at the working end to a heading cord and lashing the heading cord to the cross-bar. The following afternoon, she began weaving. She set her loom up on a grassy patch near the house with a sack underneath it. With the loom stretched between the four ground pegs, she sat bent over the loom, her skirts tucked around her crossed legs (Photo 13). The weaving progressed slowly as each weft was beaten vigorously into the fabric with a bone pick. Shed changing was a sticky business, requiring more vigorous action, and the patterns were made by hand-selecting the warps in every second row. In this way, Candelaria wove an average of four to six centimeters in each late afternoon session. For a very full description of the processes and weave structures of a similar belt (which, like Candelaria's belt, has plain weave and complementary warp weave patterns with three-span floats aligned in alternate pairs, in addition to a float weave common in Taquile fabrics), the reader is referred to Elayne Zorn's excellent article which is listed at the end.

The most distinctive products of the continuous warp, ground loom are predominantly red with white pick-up designs bordered by narrow stripes of various colors (Photo 11). From the family's store of fabrics reserved for special occasions, I was shown a number of these fabrics which ranged from *paños,* or cloths, worn at the shoulders or hips for dancing, to coca leaf bags, belts and a wedding manta. Each piece had its specific history preserved in the details of the design, colors and stripe arrangements.

To my eyes, the most arresting garment is the wide, red belt worn frequently by men (Photo 14) but also worn by women on particular occasions. Although each belt may be specific to a calendar or life event, in practice Augustin and Gonzalo often wore one of their belts day-to-day, sometimes covering it with their blue and white *chal,* or scarf. Generally, the red belts have a central pattern band about three centimeters in width, and two narrow lateral bands with traditional pick-up designs. Between these bands are stripes with float patterns of white squares on a background of red alternating with green. Narrow stripes of vivid colors flank the three figuratively patterned bands. The terminal warp area is worked into 25 or 30 three-strand braids and the warp loops are threaded onto a single re-plied cord which can double as a belt tie. The extreme width of the belt, about 17 centimeters, is held perfectly flat by a stiff underbelt which is sewn to the non-braided end of the patterned belt. The entire length of underbelt and patterned belt is wrapped continuously around the waist and fastened by tying together narrow bands or cords attached to the extremities. The narrow tying bands can be quite decorative. Gonzalo's belt ties were patterned and had tasselled ends which, on occasion, he allowed to hang at knee level. He did a twirl or two to demonstrate how attractively the tassels and ties flew when dancing.

The underbelt is made of thickly spun and plied wool or alpaca yarns, arranged in uniformly alternating stripes of light and dark. Gonzalo described how he, and other men, made the underbelts, using a frame to support the warps and a simple wrapped structure, like soumak, to produce the stiff fabric. Gonzalo said he frequently wore a red belt for daily work because the stiff underbelt gave support to his back for heavy labor.

Some warp-faced articles woven on the ground loom do not have pick-up patterns, for example, black ponchos and carrying cloths, striped *costales,* or storage sacks, and the women's brightly striped belts which are woven in a

Photo 11. Detail of Taquile warp-fabric with pick-up designs.

Photo 12. Candelaria, right, and
Pelagia warping a belt.

Photo 13. Candelaria weaving a belt
on the ground loom.

Photo 14. Men wearing warp-patterned belts in a procession at the
Fiesta of San Isidro.

heddle-controlled twill weave. The bright belts see a variety of additional uses in the swaddling of infants and in holding up the wrapped skirt of toddlers. Other warp-faced items in daily use by the family, like bags, narrow belts and small cloths used for carrying food, have only narrow pattern bands and a greater proportion of natural fleece colors.

Pelagia periodically worked on narrow warp-patterned bands, called *tesno*, which have diverse uses as bag straps, belt ties, vest decorations and wrist streamers for dancing. The bands had 36 warps and a weaving width of approximately .8 centimeter. Though the complementary weave structure is common to the ground loom fabrics, certain modifications are made to the technique for narrow bands. The shed rod is replaced by a single loop heddle which passes around all the warps that would be raised by the shed rod. The tension on the warp is not fixed but is adjustable. Pelagia body-tensioned her narrow warp in two different ways. She tied the warp to her belt and to her big toe when she wove in the stone-paved courtyard (Photo 15). Where the earth was softer, she used a peg instead of her toe. To beat in the weft, Pelagia did not use a bone pick, but instead, leaned forward, loosening the warp tension slightly, and snapped the fabric fell briskly by rocking it with her thumb and one finger which remained in the shed opening.

Photo 15. Pelagia weaving a warp-patterned band tensioned between her waist and toe.

Many designs on the bands appear to be traditional ones as they occur on other warp-patterned fabrics. A few designs are more aberrant, as though the errors of the inexperienced or inattentive had been extended into brief experiments. The bands are frequently made by girls and, though six year old Marcialina had not yet begun to weave, a nine year old cousin was weaving a band when I visited her home. It seems probable that girls learn the technique of complementary warp-patterning and the repertory of traditional designs by weaving great numbers of bands before they attempt wider fabrics.

DURING THE TIME I stayed with Faugustino's family, the Fiesta of San Isidro took place, replete with processions, dramatics and two weddings. The family did not attend the fiesta because, as members of the Adventista Church, they held apart from some of the fiestas in the almanac. They understood that I, as an outsider, was curious to see the fiesta, so I left them and followed the night procession to the village plaza. I was content on the edge of the crowd that ringed the plaza, watching the spectators more closely than the drama which dealt with themes and characters I only vaguely comprehended. In the half-light of the lamps, I had a shadowy view of the men standing at the back, like slender, identical columns, *chal* over the shoulder and *chullu* on the head.

Photo 16. The people of Taquile
watching the Fiesta of San Isidro.

Nearer the front, the women sat, amid their skirts, head after head draped by its black *chucu*, red clad arms folded or encircling a child, all intent on the drama. The repetition of silhouettes, fabrics and colors bound them together, not only in the eyes of an outsider, but as a community (Photo 16).

The fiesta continued the next day. The ribald dramatics of the night before were elaborated with new characters. At the same time, two weddings were solemnized by a Catholic priest. In the daylight, the particularities of dress of the wedding couples, the community officials and the actors were visible, though distantly. As they passed close-by, I had glimpses of unfamiliar garments, colors and patterns. I enjoyed the spectacle but knew the complexities of traditional dress used for special occasions would not be revealed to me on one short trip to Taquile.

Although I did not stay long enough to pursue the many and complex aspects of Taquile fabrics, I left feeling encouraged at the state of traditional fabric making on Taquile. Compared with other accessible parts of Peru, the fabric tradition is changing relatively slowly and the quality is remaining relatively good. Like Faugustino's family, almost all the people on the island continue to make and wear their regionally distinctive costumes, and the children continue to learn the techniques and meanings of the fabrics. The encouraging thing is that this is being done, not in isolation, but in the midst of steady contact with outsiders. Tourism is being promoted by conscious planning on a community level. Regular boat service, a rotating billet system and a cooperative store that sells island fabrics invite visitors to come, stay and buy Taquile fabrics. By periodically taking visitors into their homes and by producing fabrics for sale in excess of their own needs, families earn some necessary cash with only a modest disturbance to their lives. They appear to have arrived at the unusual, if fragile, solution whereby the cash generated by visitors encourages the continuance of a culturally integral textile art while the visitors continue to come because of these traditions. The more usual pattern is that fabrics lose both their cultural meaning and their quality as they are increasingly made for an undiscriminating tourist market.

I feel hopeful that the delicate balance that allowed me to stay with Faugustino's family and look over their shoulders while they made traditional fabrics can continue. Faugustino has no intention of changing his way of life. He plans to remain on Taquile.

The visit described took place in May, 1982. The costumes were purchased on behalf of the University of British Columbia Museum of Anthropology in Vancouver, British Columbia, and they are now part of the permanent collection of that museum.

FURTHER READING

"Warping and Weaving on a Four-stake Ground Loom in the Lake Titicaca Basin Community of Taquile, Peru" by Elayne Zorn in *1977 Proceedings, Irene Emery Roundtable on Museum Textiles: Looms and Their Products* (Washington, D.C.: The Textile Museum, 1979) describes in satisfying detail the making of a warp-patterned belt in Taquile. Elayne has produced a videotape on the same subject. She also has presented a paper, "Weaver's Rituals in Southern Peru: Before Beginning Warping", at the XLIII International Congress of the Americanists (Vancouver, 1979) that describes the rituals preceding weaving on the ground loom in Taquile.

Ann Rowe has written two works that help place the traditional, warp-patterned fabrics of Taquile in the Andean context. *Warp-Patterned Weaves of the Andes* (Washington, D.C.: The Textile Museum, 1977) describes the structures of Andean fabrics, both ancient and ethnic, which rely on warp-manipulation for patterning. "Weaving Processes in the Cuzco Area of Peru", *Textile Museum Journal*, Vol. 4, No. 2, (The Textile Museum, 1975) clarifies the distinctions among indigenous loom types in the southern Andes and gives detailed observations of weavers at work.

Jim Drum looks at the looms, both indigenous and imported, that are used today in Bolivia in "Andean Weaving Draws on the Past", *El Palacio*, Vol. 81, No. 4 (Santa Fe, 1975).

For those who wish to weave warp-patterned fabrics, *The Art of Bolivian Highland Weaving* (New York: Watson-Guptill, 1976) by Marjorie Cason and Adele Cahlander gives easy-to-follow instructions for replicating various Bolivian weaves.

TURKISH NEEDLELACE: "OYA"

BY PAT HICKMAN

Being in another land sometimes seems a solitary experience, especially if one is observing something—a textile technique such as needlelace edging—which is considered familiar and in everyone else's memory as having been around for a long time. What has been taken for granted—Turkish *oya*, known elsewhere as *bebilla*—seems to me to have great variety and beauty and a surprising perpetual freshness. Purely decorative and nonfunctional, as essential as jewelry, it is also most appealing and lively. These playful "extras", sometimes full of meaning, have been quite neglected in any serious study of Turkish textiles.

*Oya*making continues as a living tradition, still made today. *Oya* is an elaborate, precious, and intricate needlelace construction of threads, knotted. It can also mean—in a wider sense—the edging, which can be simple and direct, unpretentious, and more recently made quickly. It is, as basketry has been described by Ed Rossbach, similarly a handprocess which has *not* been mechanized, despite results which sometimes appear as uniform and anonymous as a machine product.

Though sketchy, early textile history reflecting a tradition of needlelace edging seems confirmed by the fragment of Egyptian linen netting located at the Museum of Fine Arts, Boston. In England, in the Victoria and Albert Museum collection, there is an example of edging, several different flowers on one strand, which was exhibited at the Crystal Palace in the Great Exhibition of 1851. The Royal Ontario Museum in Toronto has examples in its collection of regional 19th and 20th century costume of Greece and Bulgaria, showing an influence of Ottoman Turkish textiles and costume which, among other things, exhibit the use of needlelace edging. Turkey's present geographic boundaries clearly do not define the more widespread area—historically or today—where needlelace *oya* is, and has been, known.

Oya, then, can mean a stitch, an edging as a series of dangling flowers or other small needlenetted shapes, or a little bag. In its narrowest sense, the knotted needlelace stitch is usually made with silk thread, into an edging, on the four sides of headscarves. Unfinished raw edges of cloth are rolled under, with *oya* providing the hem, which looks very finished. Or a strand of *oya* flowers, perhaps recycled, may be attached to a separate, torn strip of cloth, later roughly stitched onto a new scarf. Scarves are replaced over and over, *oya* chains stitched on again, unimproved, unchanged borders of dangling textile flowers. Today other techniques, tatting and crochet, have been substituted for needlelace, because they can create a similar effect in much less time.

Oya is found as edging on silk shirt sleeves and necks and on little bags. The stitch can be repeated over and over to become an entire small bag by itself—for coins or a watch—not always "just" an edge.

The way an *oya*maker works is the way her mother and her grandmother worked. Generations have passed down a series of steps, the technical "know-how" remembered, repeated. We marvel that something could continue in the absence of a "how-to" paperback. An *oya*maker would not enroll in a technique workshop. Needlelace flowers developed from looking at a flower. *Oya*making has continued without sketches and diagrams, without classroom demonstrations. Increasingly, however, daughters are not inclined to learn.

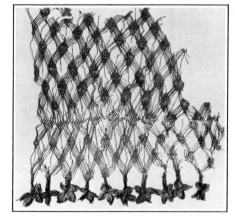

Photo 1. Linen netting. Egyptian, New Kingdom Tomb, Late Period. Lozenge design with knotted flower pendants. *Photo courtesy of Museum of Fine Arts, Boston. Gift of Mr. Stuart P. Anderson.*

Photo 2. Traditional "oya" edging on a scarf. *Collection of Buldan Seka, Berkeley.*

Photo 3. A creped silk shirt with needlelace edging. *Tire Museum Collection, Turkey.*

Photo 4. Needlelace flowers decorating a woman's headpiece from Konya, Turkey. *Collection of Kenen Özbel, Istanbul.*

Today it is hard to find women who know how to make the simplest *oya* triangular shape. In *oya*making there is not hesitating and redoing. As in knotted netting, there is no modifying or "undoing" anything, except by cutting out with scissors, once the stitch is put down and knotted (locked) in place. The traditional process requires a fine, pliable thread, a needle, and fingers moving quickly. Assured. In skilled hands performing, one is struck by the rapid movement, though the flower grows slowly. An *oya*maker has an air of confidence and authority about her. Precise workmanship is devoted to each needlelace flower. There is not a sense of immediacy or urgency. Sometimes it requires months, even years to work a strand of *oya* to its completion. A finished piece requires many starts made long before. Perhaps what is most astounding is that when done, the piece can easily be held in one hand, conveying a feeling that it deserves care and wonder. Watching an *oya*maker, there is no sensation of witnessing a creative act; at the most, a series of small decisions are made—when to change colors in a precise arrangement of color relationships, how large a unit should be. Yet it is these silent but confident decisions which determine the aesthetic quality, the visual pleasure, the *oya* shape. The whole *oya*making operation is minute, intimate, compact. It is a time experience, seemingly of an era when time was valued differently. It is so much more than the technical stitch.

Flowers, however, are built stitch by stitch, as if measured, row upon row, new stitches taking their places in relation to those already established. Openings are left between stitches. With each stitch the textile expands, until finally the chain exists, flower by flower. The *oya*maker builds these flower configurations, repeated sequences of units, measured units representing time, spacing them regularly, symmetrically in place, in precise arrangement. Between each flower shape, whether in needlelace, tatting or crochet, are alternating smaller shapes—leaves, tiny flowers, pyramid-shaped flower roots or rocks, a row of hills or mountains, a long bridge, or other geometric shapes. Sometimes this space filler seems solid from one flower to the next; other times only a single leaf or two, widely spaced between the flowers is found. This "in-between" arrangement and the flower represented can tell where the *oya* was made.

Whether in a city or a village, as an *oya*maker sat alone, her moods, her longings, her sadness is in those flowers too. *Oya* is not all dry and intellectual and cerebral but inward and introspective. These are personal expressions, notations. The *oya*maker wanted to please herself.

Obviously, I cannot speak as a traditional *oya*maker. Her observations, unrecorded, would naturally be very unlike my own. In her Islamic world, surrounded by repetition on tiled mosque domes, patterned wooden doors— with intricate geometric interlacing repeated over and over—she would expect and value repetition. In her *oya*making, an expression so small, she would be praised for work which was repetitive and unified. Her familiar cultural heritage would not especially encourage her to be inventive or innovative.

In Turkey, people's passion for flowers, their close observation of nature, has been a rich source to draw from in creating *oya* forms. An early traveler, Charles White, describes in *Three Years in Constantinople*, his account in 1846 of an Ottoman Sultan, Ahmet III, whose grand vizir, Ibrahim Pasha, a

> . . . bulbomaniac, devised new inventions to set off tulip's beauties—he illuminated [them] with thousands of small wax tapers, attached to the stems of the flowers or fixed with wires in the ground, whilst others were fastened to the backs of small tortoises, that moved constantly about among the moss and leaves, astonished at the novel purposes to which they were applied.
>
> —Vol. II, p. 46

It is indeed from a long tradition that Turks have cared so enthusiastically about flowers!

Needlelace is most commonly of familiar flowers, hundreds of species—of growth patterns closely observed—plum flowers, daisies, mimosa, even fleeting wild flowers. *Oya*makers have converted something from nature into another medium. The lack of sweet fragrance, the feel, the texture are the only clues that the "imitation" is a step removed from the real. But *oya* flowers, which in shape are their natural forms, cause one to wonder if the needlelace petals are growing or if life has just gone out of them. One doesn't think of these as artificial flowers. Some of the three dimensional *oya* flowers, stiffened, appear to be almost like miniature baskets turned over, connected together, each holding, defining, an airy volume, a netted membrane around air—nets stretched over tiny, briefly captured spaces. But they are detailed and elaborate, nonperishable flowers—not like cut flowers put into a vase without water or wild flowers gathered on a windy day, clutched and wilted before the hand stops gathering. The materials are not alive; the life quality comes when they are worn and in movement. If a scarf is worn folded over, the upper layer acts as a veil for the shifting *oya* beneath. There is a sensuous delight in wearing *oya,* in its own weightlessness, its movement in the wind, its private, almost silent sound—a pleasure in feeling more beautiful merely because of it. A toss of the head would instantly mean an exciting flutter of flowers, a multiple presentation, orchestrated single-handedly.

Photo 5. Meadow flowers. *Collection of Kenan Özbel, Istanbul.*

Photo 6. "Tombstones". *Collection of Kenan Özbel, Istanbul.*

Photo 7. "Good news" needlelace,
stuffed with dyed pink cotton
announcing pregnancy. *Collection of
Sabiha Tansuğ, Istanbul.*

Photo 8. Redpepper needlelace.
*Collection of Nimet Özmutof,
Istanbul.*

Photo 9. A young girl from Konya,
Turkey, wearing a blue scarf with
"oya" in the shape of a baby.

Photo 10. Detail of Aegean needlelace "oya". *Kenan Özbel Collection, Istanbul.*

There used to be meaning attached to *oya*, for those who understood. Without saying a word, in complete silence, a woman with her needlelace "message" could convey her own feelings, refer to her family, to something very personal. There is a long romantic tradition in Turkey of flowers being used to express a "language of love". Soon after marriage, a new bride was expected to send a gift of a scarf with *oya* edging to her mother-in-law. If all was going well, she sent one with meadow flowers—happily, evenly spaced between light and dark leaves. If the marriage was not working, a scarf with dark green finger-like projections, called "tombstones", was sent as the gift. A woman could announce that she was pregnant before it was obvious, by wearing her "good news" headscarf—tiny filled, stuffed netted forms secretly shared her surprise. If a wife and her husband were not getting along, she would wear a headscarf with small red peppers hanging from it until their argument had passed. A blue headscarf with tiny blue needlelace flowers to ward off the evil eye could be worn often by a child whose health was thought susceptible. It seems almost outrageous as an idea, the power, the message, previously understood, simply conveyed by means of distractive devices such as minute silk lace flowers. Most often the *oya* flowers are not big enough to suggest showiness or ostentation, yet they seem to be what *is* of importance.

Sophisticated city needlelace is of the finest scale, most delicate and refined. It has a preciousness, a sentimentality, an elegance. There is a paleness about it—a muted closeness in color to the scarf it's on—subtle, subdued, "dignified" color carefully chosen. There is a unity of scarf and edging most certainly felt by the maker and user. The whole piece is restrained, controlled, beautiful, and completely acceptable. Silk in *oya* holds knots securely, catching light and creating that rich, special sheen which only silk has.

By comparison with *oya* from urban centers such as Istanbul and Bursa, that from the Aegean region in southwestern Turkey seems huge. Each flower can measure 4" in the widest dimension, and in addition to scale, gives an impression of strong, bold, assertive color, most lively and playful. Wool and fleece, coarser cotton thread, bits of bright cloth, masses of felt—rougher materials clearly identifiable—are willingly used, substitutes for fine, dyed silk. Such *oya* is worn on scarves wrapped—in a very dense way—around Aegean men's headdresses. Seen this way, male presentation by a bridegroom or folk dancer, the needlelace expresses an exuberance, a vigor, an assurance.

Photo 11. Aegean men's headdress, wrapped with several scarves creating a sensation of layers thick with "oya". *Collection of Kenan Özbel, Istanbul.*

Photo 12. Bead "oya", raspberries. *Collection of Kenan Özbel, Istanbul.*

Photo 13. Foam "oya" purchased in Bursa, Turkey. *Collection of Sabiha Tansuğ, Istanbul.*

Oya seems to be as much a village as a city expression, with Anatolian villagers choosing materials readily available to them. Now, as a quick substitute for slower-made needlelace, shiny glass or plastic beads are carefully strung, arranged in patterns to resemble blackberries or raspberries, so perfectly colored and textured to be edible. There is a love of glitter, of shine, and reflections in these tiny "tassels" become dots of color. Sometimes the edging seems very heavy next to or seen through a light, sheer scarf. Village *oya*, made of these unexpected materials, has a vitality. There is an appealing innocence. What is done with each of these materials appears so obvious, so right, so inevitable. The non-silk *oya* seems more temporary and instant, not much known, seen or collected in the cities. A most playful contemporary embracing of today's materials can be seen on a scarf with foam strips cut and stitched on, flowerlike. This use of colored foam seems spontaneous, simple and direct, retaining its original identity, with no attempt to conceal or deny or elaborate with extraneous material. There is an honesty about it, a feeling that the *oya*maker enjoyed making it. *Oya* as traditional needlelace edging has changed in this innovative use of new materials—a few bits of valueless synthetic sponge, closely associated with other things, a semblance of modernity. It would be applauded by the young, bemoaned by their grandmothers—a transition almost too sudden to comprehend in a lifetime. Although the earlier exceptionally fine needlelace is no longer or very rarely being made, the old forms have not been forgotten; something of the spirit of traditional needlelace continues even in the latest creations. However, those who remember the past know with deep sadness that everything has changed around them. Older *oya*makers would not have allowed or dreamed possible the kind of improvisation, ingenuity and capriciousness exhibited in foam *oya*, so individual and adventurous. Yet they would recognize its link with a most remarkable lace past.

What seems important is that *oya* speaks of time, of all time rather than of its present moment. That *oya* has been expressive of a culture seems significant, and that there was an audience which valued *oya*. The traditional value and meaning, intimately known, is someone else's; we are denied that experience. But perhaps in trying to understand some of the original essence or spirit of *oya*, including its change, by feeling its "time", its appropriateness to the total life, its unpretentiousness, our own awareness of the human experience is expanded. A brief moment has connected with another culture, another tradition, with its textile art, with Turkish *oya*.

From: Hickman, Pat. *Turkish Oya*, M.A. Thesis, Design Department, University of California, Berkeley 1977.

Among many others whom I came to know and who helped me see and love and enjoy oya, I am especially grateful to Sabiha Tansuğ for her generous sharing, for the opportunity of studying and working with her in Turkey.

BIBLIOGRAPHY

Arseven, Celal E. *Les Arts Decoratifs Turcs.* Istanbul: Milli Eğitim Basimevi, 1952.

Bath, Virginia Churchill. *Lace.* Chicago: Henry Regnery Company, 1974.

Caulfield, S.F.A. *Encyclopedia of Victorian Needlework*, Vol. II. New York: Dover Publications, Inc., 1972.

Dillmont, Thérèse de. *The Complete Encyclopedia of Needlework.* Philadelphia: Running Press, 1972.

Gilroy, Clinton G. *The Art of Weaving.* London: Wiley & Putnam, 1845.

Halsband, Robert, ed. *Complete Letters of Lady Mary Wortley Montagu*, Vol. I-III. Oxford: Clarendon Press, 1967.

Kay-Shuttleworth, R.B. "Lace VI. Needle-Made Laces", *Embroidery*, The Journal of the Embroiderers' Guild, London, Vol. VII, no. 3, Autumn, 1956. Pp. 84-86.

Maynard, B.W. "Armenian Needlepoint", *Embroidery*, Vol. II, no. 1, Spring, 1951. Pp. 22-24.

Özbel, Kenan. *Türk El Sanatlar*, Ankara: C.H.P. Halkevleri Burosu, 1940.

Onuk, Taciser. *Needleworks.* Türk Tarih Kurumu Basimevi, Ankara, 1981.

Tansuğ, Sabiha. "The Langauge of Flowers II", *Sanat Dünyamiz.* Yapi ve Kredi Bankasi, Jan. 1979.

-----. "Turkey", *Love and Marriage, Aspects of Folk Life in Europe, 1975.* Musée de la Vie Wallonne, Liège, 1975. Pp. 273-280.

Wardle, Patricia. *Victorian Lace.* London: Frederick A. Praeger, 1968.

White, Charles. *Three Years in Constantinople.* London: Henry Colburn, Publ., 3 Vols., 1846.

RESERVED SHED
PEBBLE WEAVE IN PERU

BY ED M. FRANQUEMONT

During the first half of 1978 we were contracted by the Compania de Minas Buenaventura of Lima, Peru, to survey the part of the Dept. of Huancavelica, Peru, where they based their mining operations. We were looking for any products that could be exported to provide jobs and income for craftspeople, artisans, or the general folk of the area. Our search became in part a survey of textile skills, textile production, and the availability of the raw products on which they depend. The research reported in this paper is the direct result not only of Buenaventura's generous support of our work, but also of their foresight and social responsibility in attempting to improve the economic conditions for people who were in no direct way connected to their mining enterprise. During the course of our survey we came across an interesting weaving system that we had not seen before, a semi-loom controlled kind of "Pebble Weave" that accomplishes complex pick-up patterns quickly and easily. This paper describes our encounter with the man who taught us reserved shed pebble weaving, some of the principles on which it is based, and the character of the design sense that results.

Photo A. A band of three color pebble weave from Chinchero.

We were taught to weave *chumpis,* or belts, by Lucio Arechi, a 50 year old professional weaver from the town of Callanmarca, near Lircay, Huancavelica, Peru. We had visited Lucio several times previously, and knew that, like most professional weavers in the area, he is one of the poorest men in town. He turned to weaving early in his life when he realized that his holdings of land and animals would not be sufficient to support him and his family, and actively set about learning to weave from some of his kinsmen who knew how. He works for the most part under the contract system that prevails in Huancavelica; under its terms, a wealthier man will contract with some poor person to spin his fleece into yarn and then will contract with Lucio or some other weaver to make the cloth. The weaver never actually owns the cloth on which he works, and earns so little for his labor that he is generally unable to invest in the materials necessary to his work. Average pay for a weaver's day in 1978 was about s/40 (about US 25¢). The result is that the weavers of the area work only to fill the domestic demand of their wealthier neighbors, and there is no surplus of cloth produced that might be used for sale. The weavers themselves enter the trade because of poverty, and seldom escape despite years of hard work and great technical skill.

Lucio Arechi taught us to weave according to a system of weaving that we had not seen during our years with the weavers of Chinchero in the Dept. of Cuzco. The skills of *chumpi* weaving are not a prelude to work on the large backstrap loom as they are in Chinchero, but rather a wholly separate series of skills and understandings. We met many people who could weave ponchos on the large backstrap loom but did not know how to make *chumpis* at all. Large loom weaving seems to be exclusively the province of men in Huancavelica, but many women and some men weave belts. We had a hard time finding someone to teach us the belt techniques until we happened to run into Lucio, who for a small sum of money (s/100) gladly passed onto us the skills he had learned from his kinsmen years earlier. He said that he would use the same teaching technique by which he had learned ("Qhawaspa, Qhawaspa". . . watching, watching) and did little explanation of what he was about, although he did take greater pains to show us what he considered important than do most Chinchero weavers in similar circumstances.

Lucio brought out a lovely *chumpi* of orange and white with a blue border and asked if we wanted one like that. We quickly assented, and he noted that we lacked enough white yarn to make the warp. We set about plying some that we had brought, and finally talked him into transposing the colors so that we could work with the yarns we had. His warping tools consisted of two end points and nothing more; one was a large nail but the other was a wooden stake about 10" long. We had never seen such a stake before but had always suspected that this sort of thing must have been used in the days before large steel nails were available, so we pressed him for a name. "This?" he said with surprise. "It's called a stake (*Estaca*)". By this time we were used to feeling foolish after asking the name of weaving equipment, since we had had similar experiences in Chinchero. Lucio wound the warp in a simple figure eight pattern on these two end points that left an elongated cross in the middle (Photo 1). He wound the edging and three border stripes of a single yarn, and switched to two threads of contrasting colors when he began the pattern section. He demonstrated to us that this first design band consisted of six such pairs of threads counted along one lease, for a total of 24 warp ends, 12 of each color. Because of the two colors taken through the warping pattern together, one-half of the threads in each lease are of one color and the other half are of the contrasting color. When the winding of the warp on the frame was completed, it appeared as shown in Figure 1A. Lucio tied the warp in three places—at both ends and around the cross. He tied the near end where the weaving was to begin with a heavy four-strand cord. Next he tied the far end of the warp with a shorter doubled thread of the same yarns, and finally he tied a doubled thread of a single contrasting color around the cross. When the warp was secure, he removed it from the pegs.

Before tying himself into the warp, Lucio prepared five sticks to be used in the weaving. He was careful that the first of these be of dry wood and strong, but the others were all cut from the green stalks of the common weeds that were growing in his dooryard. He mumbled apologetically that the green wood was really not good for some of the sticks, but they would do; if we wished we could change them later. The first dry stick, about 5" long and virtually straight, was to serve as a loom bar. In Chinchero it would be called a *kakina*, but we were unable to get a Huancavelica name. The second stick, the *karpucha*, was to act as two lease rods to hold the cross. It had two legs of equal size and length. Lucio trimmed the *karpucha* with care to remove the main stalk without weakening the joint between the two legs. The third stick, also green and forked, became a holding stick. There was one leg longer than the warp was wide and one short little leg that resembled a hook. The fourth and fifth sticks, the *illawacha* (diminuitive of the word for heddle), were identical and became the heddle rods. Lucio broke the *illawachas* in their

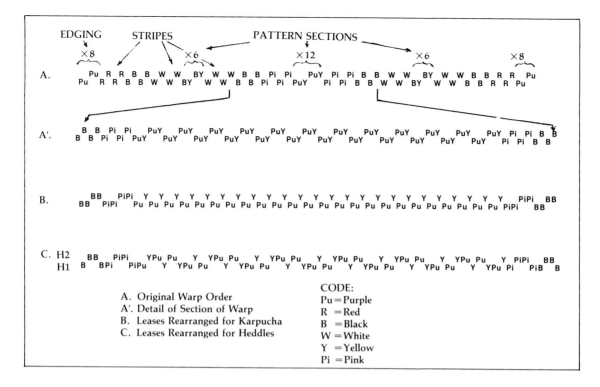

CODE:
Pu = Purple
R = Red
B = Black
W = White
Y = Yellow
Pi = Pink

Figure 1. Warp orders and rearrangements.

centers, leaving a piece of green stem as a hinge about which the stick could be doubled back upon itself.

When these five sticks were ready, Lucio lashed the far end of the warp to a large upright house support. He put the first stick through the warp loops at the near end and tucked the ends of the stick into his belt so that the warp was firmly attached to his middle. He put the second stick, the *karpucha*, through the cross with a leg of the stick on either side of the cross (Photo 2). Using this cross as a guide to the sequence of yarns, Lucio manipulated the threads with his left hand and rearranged them into two new leases on the first two fingers of his right hand. The new cross that resulted had the sequence of threads shown in Figure 1B, with the edging threads left in their original order and the stripe threads put into doubled pairs. The yarns of the pattern sections were rearranged so that contrasting color yarns fell into different leases. When this rearrangement was completed, the *karpucha* was removed from the warping cross and reinserted into the newly formed cross. The open ends of the legs of the *karpucha* were tied tightly together so that the stick could not fall out during weaving.

Another rearrangement of the yarns followed, this time to form the leases on which the heddles were to be applied. Lucio accomplished this in the same manner as before, following the sequence of yarns in the new cross now held on the *karpucha* and manipulating the yarns with his left hand to form two new leases on the first two fingers of his right hand. These new heddle leases had the sequence shown in the detail of Figure 1C. He again kept the yarns of the edging in their original order and put the yarns of the stripe sections into pairs, but this time he staggered the sequence of yarns in the pairs. In both *karpucha* leases the paired threads of the stripe sections were always of the same color (Fig. 1B); in one of the heddle leases, the pairs had yarns of different colors (Fig. 1C). The yarns of the pattern sections were rearranged into an irregular order as shown in Figure 1C. This irregular order is well known from the Andes and can be written in shorthand as ABBABAAB. This means that the first thread of the warp is placed on Heddle 1 (A), the second and third regardless of color are placed as a pair on Heddle 2 (B), the fourth thread on

Photo 1. Making the warp.

Photo 2. The *karpucha* in place.

Photo 3. Heddles.

Photo 4. Using the shed sword.

Photo 5. Pick-up at the *karpucha*.

Photo 6. A mixed-color reserved shed in storage.

Photos 1-6 of Lucio Arechi at work, 1978.

Heddle 1 (A), the fifth on Heddle 2 (B), and the sixth and seventh are placed as a pair on Heddle 1 (A), and the eighth on Heddle 2 (B). Lucio put these two new leases onto temporary holding sticks and then tied each onto a separate heddle, using the *illawacha* as heddle rods.

The heddle rods were sticks that had been partially broken in the center so that they could be doubled back upon themselves. Lucio used the end of the heddle cord to tie the two halves of one stick together with a figure eight. He opened one of the heddle leases and pushed the stick with the heddle cord back through the open lease to the right side of the warp, and laid it on top of the warp (Photo 3). The threads of the lease to be tied onto the heddle were held above the heddle cord and below the heddle rod. The heddle loops themselves were made by picking the heddle cord up to the left of each warp, but the cord was put onto the rod in such a way that half the loops fell in front of the rod and half behind. There were two planes to the heddle, which may help in shedding a closely sett warp or may be a purely cultural variable. Lucio repeated the procedure to install the second heddle on the remaining lease from the final rearrangement of the warp yarns.

As Lucio began to weave, he had the hooked holding stick by his side with a single broad, short shed sword, and a small butterfly of weft yarn. He inserted the shed sword into the separation just in front of the *karpucha*, and turned it on edge to raise the lease with a purple design band in the center. He dropped all of the purple edging threads and reinserted the shed sword and the hooked holding stick in the lease. Turning the shed sword on edge once again, he agitated the warp in front of the heddles with his thumbs to clear the shed past the heddles to the front of the warp, and then passed the first weft. For the second pick, he raised one of the heddles by relaxing tension on the warp and pulling the heddles in opposite directions. Lucio grasped a heddle rod in each hand and pulled one up and to the left while he pulled the other down and to the right. He slipped his little finger into the space between the heddle sheds and dropped the heddle rods. He inserted the shed sword in place of his little finger, turned it on edge and cleared the heddle shed forward to the woven edge (Photo 4). The third pick was identical to the first and came from the holding stick. For the fourth pick, Lucio raised the second heddle and brought it forward. This series of motions produced a pebble field that was purple with yellow pebbles in the central design band. To make a solid color-effect field of the contrasting color yellow, Lucio returned to the *karpucha*, dropped the purple threads and manually picked up the yellow lease (Photo 5) that was held on the far side of the *karpucha* and placed it on the holding stick. Weaving proceeded in the same four steps—holding stick, heddle 1, holding stick, heddle 2—but with the yellow lease on the holding stick, a yellow field with purple pebbles resulted.

By this point we had gathered how the patterns were done, but Lucio showed us anyway. Working from the *karpucha*, he manually picked up a lease that was part purple and part yellow (Photo 6). This was placed on the holding stick and brought forward as a shed and woven. The heddle sheds were handled in precisely the same manner as before, but the result was a field of one color imposed upon a background of the other. Lucio changed the pattern by changing the constitution of the shed held on the holding stick. He was free to change these patterns in many different ways but seemed to favor S-shapes and zigzag lines with pendant diamonds.

The weave that Lucio Arechi taught us is a complementary warp weave well known from both contemporary and ancient Andean contexts. In *Warp-Patterned Weaves of the Andes*, Ann Rowe emphasizes the tremendous variety of complementary warp weaves, the ease with which a weaver can move from one interlacing order to another, and the difficulties of subdividing the class of complementary warp weaves further (Rowe, Ch. 10, esp. p. 67). Lucio's belt weave underscores these observations. The equipment is designed to produce fields of three span floats aligned in alternate pairs easily and quickly (such fields are illustrated in Figs. 2 and 3). Pairs of warps float over three picks of weft and are tied down under one weft before they float again, and these pairs are staggered so that the tie downs for adjacent pairs never occur in the same row. Where a pair of warps is tied down, a pair of contrasting color warps are visible as the pebbles of an otherwise solid color field. These pebbles are *ñawi*, or eyes, to Quechua weavers who see in them a parallel to the eyes of their staple food, the potato. North American sources have called the tie downs pebbles (for example, Birrell, *The Textile Arts*, pp. 140-143), and while the term Pebble Weave does not adequately describe the structure of the weave, the design potential of the weave is vast and the structure itself quite variable. In many of the patterns drafted here, the basic scheme of three span floats aligned in alternate pairs does not even appear (see Fig. 6), although the equipment is designed to produce this effect. Since the purpose of this paper is to report an unusual weaving procedure, not to examine the structure of the fabric, I use the term Pebble Weave loosely to include any weave that is based on pebble rows in which colors alternate in pairs.

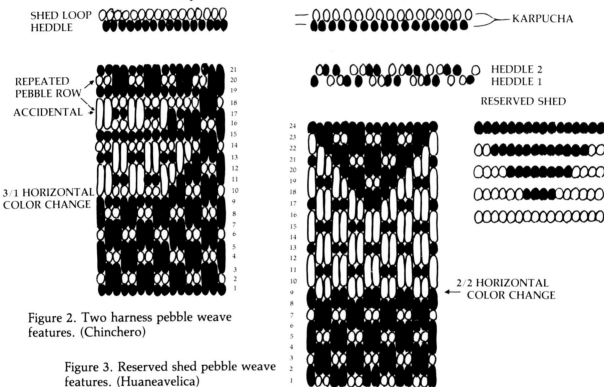

Figure 2. Two harness pebble weave features. (Chinchero)

Figure 3. Reserved shed pebble weave features. (Huaneavelica)

Rowe (*loc. cit.*) has a thorough description of the structure of this and other related complementary warp weaves; but it is worth reviewing here her observations about the two ways Andean weavers change the color of pebble weave fields, because they seem to be related to the method of manufacture. The weaver accomplishes "3/1 Horizontal Color Change" by weaving two successive picks of plain weave in contrasting colors (Fig. 2, picks #9 and #10). This produces a horizontal (or weft-wise) stripe of one color followed immediately by a horizontal stripe of the contrasting color with no row of pebbles in between. It is called "3/1 Horizontal Color Change" because pairs of three span floats alternate with pairs of single span yarns on both sides of the color change. The "2/2 Horizontal Color Change" (Fig. 3, pick #9) has a row of pebbles between the picks of plain weave of contrasting color. The result is pairs of two span floats of alternate color at the color change.

The accompanying diagrams are representations of one face of the pattern sections of the cloth. Except for Figure 1, stripes and edging threads have been left out of the diagrams. On the opposite face of the cloth, the colors occupy reverse positions. Beside each pattern diagram I have included the composition of the reserved sheds held on the holding stick, and for multi-stick patterns indicated the number of the sticks in use. Figure 1A depicts the entire warp made by Lucio Arechi, including the colors of the yarns and their locations. In Figures 1A', B and C, the central portion of this warp is reproduced in larger scale for clarity.

Lucio Arechi's method is the second we have learned for pebble weaving. The artisans of Chinchero use a two-harness system that requires extensive pick-up to form not only the pattern sheds but even the basic solid color effect fields. The loom is warped and the heddle is installed in an ABAB order so that one lease controls all of the yarns of a single color while the other shedding device carries the contrasting color. This arrangement is shown at the top of Figure 2. The plain weave that results from alternating the two shedding devices consists of alternating horizontal (weft-wise) stripes. To construct a pebble field with a solid color effect, the weaver "picks pebbles" on the lease opposite the field color. To form a black field with white pebbles the weaver takes the black lease directly as it comes from the shedding device without pick-up; this results in a solid stripe of black. On the next pick, when the white lease is up facing the weaver, she drops every other pair of white threads and picks up their black partners. On the third pick she repeats the plain weave in black, while on the fourth she drops the white pairs that had been held on the second pick and picks up their partners. The solid color pebble field that results from this work is indistinguishable from that produced by Lucio's system, but is achieved by picking up half of the threads of the warp on every other pick of weft. This involves substantially more finger manipulation than the loom controlled weave from Huancavelica.

Chinchero weavers using the two-harness system of pebble weave produce patterns by a much different process than their Huancavelica counterparts. They favor figure ground motifs that are constructed by placing a field of one color within the background of the contrasting color, which allows a design potential similar to eight-harness double cloth. The current favorite patterns involve mounted horsemen, birds, menageries of fanciful beasts and even some historical themes. In practice, the weaver works from the woven edge, making up patterns as she goes, adapting others to fit the thread count, and adding embellishments as desired. In each case, she bears in mind what she has just completed, plans her next pick-up by direct visual inspection, and executes the work on a pick by pick basis. Every pick of the pattern contains part of the background field and part of the figure which is rendered in the contrasting color. When the black lease is up facing the weaver, she leaves the plain weave in the black field sections of the pattern but picks pebbles in the white field sections; when the white lease is up, she leaves the plain weave white in the white field sections and picks pebbles in the black zones. This means that the Chinchero weaver picks up somewhere for every shot of weft except in those few places where the entire warp is a solid color. She lays her work out from the vertical or diagonal boundaries between color zones and places the pebbles in alternating pairs as needed to fill the space. In most cases, the pebbles of the black sections are not on the same schedule as those of the white section since they are laid out independently and do not occur in the same pick. The pairs of pebbles might begin on the odd numbered thread in the black section (e.g., 3 & 4, 5 & 6, 7 & 8, etc.) and on the even numbered threads in the white (e.g., 20 & 21, 22 & 23, 24 & 25, etc.). Occasionally, the identical pebble pick-up may even be repeated twice around a horizontal color change (Fig. 2, pick #13). This causes no damage to the structure of the fabric because these weavers employ a 3/1 horizontal color change in which successive picks of plain weave tie down all the threads.

The essential features of the Chinchero method of pebble weaving are the use of two harnesses, pick-up of pebbles somewhere on every shot of weft, a non-standardized pebble schedule, and a 3/1 horizontal color change between color zones. While these features suggest that the method of work might be inferred from the finished cloth or the weaving apparatus, it is equally interesting to observe the design sense that the technology encourages in the weaver. There is a freedom here that is quite remarkable for Andean weavers

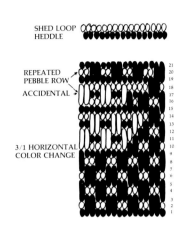

SHED LOOP
HEDDLE

REPEATED
PEBBLE ROW
ACCIDENTAL

3/1 HORIZONTAL
COLOR CHANGE

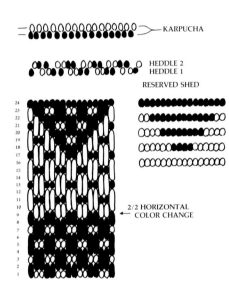

KARPUCHA

HEDDLE 2
HEDDLE 1

RESERVED SHED

2/2 HORIZONTAL
COLOR CHANGE

Figures 2 and 3 are repeated here for close proximity to the text.

who are accustomed to the more rigidly defined patterns; some of our older friends in Chinchero who are excellent weavers in their own style have had a difficult time adjusting to the personal creativity allowed by the pebble weaves that have appeared in their village over the past 20 years. The artist proficient in the style of weaving can produce almost any shape field desired and therefore virtually any motif that she can imagine, although there are of course some designs that are currently in vogue among all weavers and some weavers who spend their lives repeating the same few pebble weave motifs. Whether they are made by limited or more accomplished craftspeople, however, most of the patterns used by these weavers are large figure ground motifs that are asymmetrical in both the warp-wise and the weft-wise directions. Talented and creative weavers frequently even use accidentals to achieve grace and fluidity in the pattern (Fig. 2, pick #17). In these places, the standard alternation of the pebble pairs is changed to accommodate the pattern with no loss of structure. A pebble sequence of 2B, 2W, 2B, 2W, etc., might be changed to 2B, 3W, 2B, etc., or to 2B, 1W, 1B, 2W, etc. The technology of the two-harness pebble weave (while much slower and more labor intensive than the semi-loom controlled version from Huancavelica) encourages a fluid and creative design sense that tends to express itself in asymmetrical figure ground motifs. These stand in sharp contrast to most of the abstract patterns that dominate most of Chinchero weaving.

The reserved shed pebble weaving that Lucio Arechi taught us in 1978 differs from the Chinchero method not only in terms of the equipment employed but also in the repetitive small scale symmetrical design sense that is encouraged and the way the weaver works the pattern. It is a semi-loom controlled weave in that the pebble rows do not ever have to be picked up manually by the weaver. Every other row throughout the design panel is always a pebble row, and because the pebbles are produced by the heddles, they are everywhere on the same schedule regardless of the color of the zone they happen to appear in. At the outset of the weaving, the weaver establishes the odd or even numbered rows as the pebble rows, and this remains constant throughout the cloth (Fig. 3). The intervening rows are the pattern rows where all color change takes place and all pattern decisions are made. In effect, the weaver has reduced by half the number of picks in which he must make decisions and do pick-up, and can mentally factor out all of the pebble rows from design consideration.

By adroit use of the reserved shed principle and clever design, the weaver can further simplify the construction of a complex pattern and escape even more work. All pattern decisions and pick-up are done at the *karpucha* behind the heddles during the formation of the pattern sheds. Except during the weaving of a solid color-effect field, these pattern picks held on the holding stick are mixed in color and contain some threads from the front of the *karpucha* and some from the back. Most patterns are laid out so that each pattern pick can be formed directly from the one before it without counting and frequently without even having to refer to the woven edge or the developing pattern itself. Figure 3, picks #17-#24, show how to generate an opening diamond shape in the center of a solid color-effect field.

The first pattern shed has four black colored threads in the center of an otherwise white pattern shed. The next pattern shed drops two white threads on either side of the black zone and adds their partners. The third pattern pick (which is the fifth pick of this sequence overall) drops two more white threads on either side of the black zone and picks up their black partners, and the weaving continues according to this principle. The procedure encourages the weaver to think of patterns as a series of principles that act at the *karpucha* rather than as a series of picks that happen at the woven edge. Some of the principles are really quite simple, easy to understand and easy to express in words and yet produce some seemingly complex designs. With this system of work, there is no need to memorize pattern drafts, count large numbers, or use higher math to generate typically lovely Andean patterns.

Figure 4 shows several one-stick patterns that can be used with the pebble weave heddles to create a complex design. For each of these patterns, the weaver forms the pattern shed at the *karpucha* and places it in reserve on a holding stick before bringing the shed through the heddles to be woven; these pattern sheds are shown to the right of the pattern. The weaver raises one of the heddles and passes a weft on the pebble row. When he returns to the *karpucha* to form a second pattern shed, he removes the holding stick, re-forms the pattern lease on his hand and re-inserts the holding stick before bringing the pattern shed through the heddles to be woven. Each pattern shed is formed from the one before but is unique in that it is woven only once before it is disassembled. The holding stick keeps the pattern pick in storage while it and the following pebble row are being woven, but the pattern shed itself is used only for reference in forming the next pick. The *ñawi-ñawi* all-over diamond motif shown in Figure 4, rows 1-12, is unusual because the pattern shed once formed may be used a second time before it is disassembled. Pattern picks 2 and 4 are identical, as are 6 and 8, and 10 and 12. Here the fortunate weaver need only pick up for every fourth shot of weft, a considerable savings of time and energy. The principle at work here involves a pattern shed that alternates colors in four warp blocks across the web. In the second set of pattern picks (6 and 8), the colors change location. This can be expressed as "alternate blocks of four alternating positions". But there is even more simplification of the process possible by thinking of the pattern as a two-stick pattern that requires two holding sticks. The first pattern is formed, placed on the holding stick, and woven twice (alternating of course with the appropriate heddle sheds). The second pattern pick is formed easily by inspection from the first by dropping all threads in favor of their partners. But to speed the work, the weaver leaves the first pattern pick on a holding stick and inserts the second holding stick in the second pattern pick in front of the first. He then weaves the second pattern shed twice. Pattern picks 10 and 12 use the same array of yarns as pattern picks 2 and 4, and this warp configuration is still being held on the first holding stick. To retrieve it, the weaver simply removes the second holding stick and brings the first one forward to be woven twice. The second pattern pick now must be re-formed by pick-up from the first. By using two holding sticks and the reserved principle, the weaver has arrived at a situation where he can execute the *ñawi-ñawi* pattern by picking up only once for every eight shots of weft.

Figure 4. One-stick patterns.

Figure 5 shows a series of two-stick patterns that are faster and easier to do than the one-stick patterns because they require substantially less pick-up. The parallel line and diamond motifs of picks 1-18 are similar to four-harness twills, but the *mujercita* of picks 21-38 shows how the two-stick principle can be extended to create more free-form patterns with advantage. The reserved sheds used to make these patterns are shown to the right of the design along with indications of the alternation of the various sticks and heddles. In some places, only one holding stick is used.

More complex and longer patterns can be achieved with the use of more reserved sheds held on more holding sticks. In Figure 6, I have drafted *mayo k'enko*, the meandering river pattern in wide use in contemporary Peru and Bolivia. It can be done with four holding sticks. The pattern sheds of picks 4, 6, 8 and 10 are formed in their turns and stored on holding sticks. Each pattern pick is woven and then pushed back out of the way toward the *karpucha* so that the subsequent pattern shed may be formed from it, woven and then pushed back. After pick number 10 is formed, woven, and put into storage, there are four holding sticks in the warp between the *karpucha* and the heddles. Pattern shed 10, being the last woven, is closest to the heddles and the weaver, while number 4 is the furthest away. On the return of the pattern after pick 11 the weaver has a free ride and need do no further pick-up. He retrieves each pattern shed out of storage in reverse sequence to the way they were put in, using pattern shed number 10 to weave pick number 12, shed number 8 to weave pick 14, pattern shed 6 for pick 16 and finally pattern shed 4 to weave

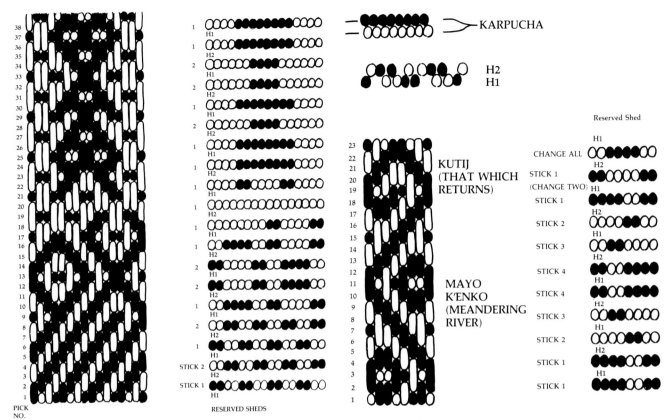

Figure 5. Two-stick patterns.

Figure 6. Multi-stick patterns.

pick 18. In this way the weaver is able to weave twice with each pattern shed and can accomplish the *mayo k'enko* pattern by picking up for only one quarter of the shots of weft. The design that results is of course symmetrical from top to bottom but not necessarily symmetrical from side to side. Since the picks placed in storage are exact copies of those woven earlier, not only is this symmetry absolute, but also any errors that were committed during the first half of the design are reproduced exactly in the second. Such repeating errors probably indicate that reserved shed principles were used.

Mayo k'enko is a simple pattern with few threads and an alternating side-to-side symmetry, but it is a good example of the advantages of the reserved shed principle. The same pattern can be rendered with more warps by adding more holding sticks or doubling the pattern to be bilaterally symmetrical. In my own work, I have used as many as 14 holding sticks, which allow quite complex patterns and long symmetries. Andean weavers develop other complex patterns without adding more equipment by exercising the freedom they have to alter the reserved sheds as they come out of storage. Very minor pick-up on the reserved sheds can transform the *mayo k'enko* pattern to *kutij* ("That which returns"), as shown in Figure 6, picks 17-23. In fact, almost any pebble weave pattern, including the large asymmetrical figure ground motifs of the Cuzco area, can be adapted to a heddle and holding stick system. The finished cloth is characterized by the consistent all-over layout of the pebble rows and a 2/2 horizontal color change in which the rows of plain weave that change the color of the section are separated by a row of pebbles. These patterns, however, do not use the equipment and technology of the loom to its best advantage because the ability to store sheds is of more limited value and the weaver is required to consult the woven edge frequently to determine the next pick-up. This is more trouble than it sounds, because two heddles stand between the woven edge and the *karpucha* where the pick-up is to be made, and it is difficult to identify the proper threads for pick-up. The belts we saw in Huancavelica in 1978 were in fact almost exclusively made of reciprocal top-to-bottom symmetrical designs with only minor changes in the reserved sheds.

These weavers have come to recognize and employ abstract principles along with their distinctive loom set-up to produce Andean pebble weave patterns quickly and easily.

Although Chinchero weavers do not know how to pebble weave with Lucio Arechi's method, they are familiar with the reserved shed principle from the tubular edgings that adorn their *llicllas* and ponchos. In a recent issue of *The Weaver's Journal,* Cahlander, Franquemont and Bergman describe how this is done and illustrate the equipment. Photo 7 here shows a tubular edging in progress with the forked stick and holding stick in place. This is a crossed warp weave, so the use of the reserved shed is especially helpful because any errors made in the crossings automatically right themselves when the shed is retrieved from storage. It must be significant that these two diverse and widely separated applications of the reserved shed principle both employ the forked lease rod and holding stick, but it is difficult to fathom what it means. It is hard to imagine that one is derived from the other in any way; perhaps there was, or even still is, a more generalized technology that used this equipment in a number of unusual ways.

It is difficult to know whether other people in the Andes are using the reserved shed principle to make pebble weaves, since we lack firsthand ethnographic information or diagnostic tools that would allow identification of the process from the finished product. Row (*op. cit.* p. 69) notes several different warp orders in use to produce complementary warp weaves, including the irregular ABBABAAB warp order that Lucio Arechi uses for his heddles, but it is difficult to know whether or not this implies the use of the reserved shed. Cason and Cahlander (*The Art of Bolivian Highland Weaving,* pp. 83-85) report an irregular warp order from Bolivia, but suggest that the pattern picks are formed by pick-up from these irregular heddles themselves. Rowe also illustrates a number of pieces of cloth that have 2/2 horizontal color change like that found in Huancavelica. These are from both ancient and modern contexts, including several from the Department of Cuzco. While the 2/2 horizontal color change may indicate some sort of loom control over the pebble rows, there is no reason to assume that reserved shed principles must be at work as well.

Photo 7. A tubular edging being woven, with the forked stick and holding stick in place.

Several promising lines of research suggest themselves. Analytical studies may be able to develop a way of looking at the finished cloth to determine method of manufacture, which may reveal something about the antiquity and distribution of reserved shed pebble weaving. Further field work in the Andes may be able to pin down the distribution of this weaving system in the highlands, or even uncover a larger textile technology based on the forked lease rod and the reserved shed principle. But it is difficult to use either Chinchero or Huancavelica evidence to know which direction to turn next. Chinchero people are regarded by their neighbors as a people apart from the rest of Cuzco, and this view is supported by many of their social customs, including a distinctive hairstyle for women. For over 300 years, the mercury mines of Huancavelica were a vortex that pulled people from the entire southern highlands of Peru and left them to form a cultural amalgam that is today deeply marked by Spanish vaquero ideas. In such an area, it may be difficult to trace the history of the ingenuity, inspiration, and aesthetic development that the weaving of Lucio Arechi represents.

BIBLIOGRAPHY

Birrell, Verla. *The Textile Arts.* New York: Schocken Books, 1973.
Cahlander, Adele, Ed Franquemont and Barbara Bergman. "A Special Andean Tubular Trim— Woven Without Heddles", in *The Weaver's Journal.* Vol. VI, No. 3, Issue 23 (Winter 1981-82), pp. 54-58.
Cason, Marjorie and Adele Cahlander. *The Art of Bolivian Highland Weaving.* New York: Watson-Guptill, 1976.
Rowe, Ann Pollard. *Warp-Patterned Weaves of the Andes.* Washington, D.C.: The Textile Museum, 1977.

Photo 1. A pouch with a panel of animals executed in quillwork on leather. A pouch measures 28.5cm×15.2cm, and it is decorated with white beads, conical tin ornaments, and two kinds of trade cloth. *Courtesy of the Denver Art Museum. 1955.199.*

Photo 2. Detail of Photo 1.

DERIVATIVE WORK BASED ON PORCUPINE QUILL EMBROIDERY

BY VIRGINIA ISHAM HARVEY

Porcupines are native to most of Canada, but they are found in the United States only along the west slope of the Cascades in Washington and Oregon, on both sides of the Rocky Mountains, in the states bordering the Great Lakes and continuing east along the Canadian border to Maine. Quillwork has been attributed not only to the areas where the animals are found, but also to many of the Plains Indians, so they must have either traded for quills or made excursions to areas where porcupines lived.

The porcupine furnished both quills and food for the Indians. First, the quills were plucked and graded into four sizes. The largest quills, which came from the tail, were used for wrapping fringes or the handles of tools. A medium size was plucked from the back, and a smaller size from the neck. The smallest quills came from the underside of the animal, and these were used for the finest embroidery. Porcupine was considered a delicacy, so after it was plucked, it was cooked and eaten.

The Indian women prepared the quills and embroidered costumes, accessories, tools, sheaths, and other items with them. Until aniline dyes were available, the quills were dyed with natural materials. After they were dyed and allowed to dry, sometimes they were rubbed with bear oil to give them a gloss.

The patterns for the quillwork were marked on soft, tanned leather with a bone marker. Sometimes the leather was rubbed to mark it, other times patterns were painted with soft earth colors made of mud or other natural materials. An awl was used to pierce the holes for sewing, and sinew was usually used to attach the quills to leather. The embroiderers either put the quills in water or held them in their mouths to soften them, then they pulled them through their teeth or used a thumbnail to flatten them. A few bone instruments have been found that may have been used to flatten the quills as the embroidery progressed, but it is more likely that these tools were used to rub over the embroidery for a final flattening and smoothing after it was completed.

Sometimes quills were woven into narrow bands or braided, then attached for decoration or wrapped on something like a knife handle. Whether the quills were woven or embroidered, each quill was added to the work individually. A quill was worked into a design tip first, and because a quill is hollow like the quill of a feather, the next quill tip could be slipped into the hollow base of the previous quill. Thus the quills formed a continuous line as the work progressed.

In this article, we will be concerned only with several of the methods used to attach the quills directly to leather. The methods the Indian women used can be adapted for contemporary work to ribbons, strips of fabric or leather

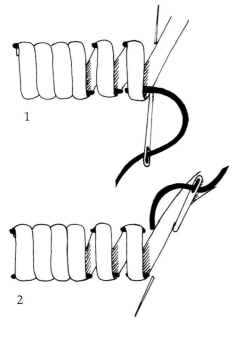

1

2

3

fastened either on a fabric or a leather background. Photo 3 is embroidered with quillwork techniques using grosgrain ribbon. For variety, some of the ribbons were fastened in place with a decorative couching that is not a quillwork technique. Photo 4 is a combination of traditional embroidery stitches and leather strips attached with quillwork techniques.

One of the quillwork techniques used in Photo 4 resembles a band of traditional satin stitch embroidery; however, its execution is more complicated than satin stitch. Figures 1 and 2 demonstrate the steps used to fasten the quills to the surface. In both of these diagrams, and in other illustrations that explain variations of this technique, the last two vertical strips are placed with space between them to show the process of attaching them. Normally, these strips would fit together like the first few strips, and none of the stitches would be visible. Also, the beginning part of the strip shows in Figure 1 to illustrate the beginning of the attachment. This end should be tucked under the work, as shown in Figure 2 and other similar diagrams.

Stitches as long as the width of the material to be attached to the background are placed over each fold as the work progresses. To begin this band of design, attach the beginning of the strip with the stitch shown in Figure 2. When the strip is attached at the top, either as the work begins or for any of the other stitches at the top of the band, the holding stitch goes over the strip as it is extended on the background as shown in Figure 2. The stitch is pulled down firmly, and then the strip is folded over the holding stitch. Attaching the lower edge of the stitch differs because the strip is folded first, then the thread goes under the fold but over the extended strip as shown in Figure 1. The fold is adjusted as the holding stitch is tightened. The reverse side of Figure 2 is shown in Figure 3. Moving from top to bottom with the stitching as the strip is attached leaves long floats of the stitching thread on the back of the work. The dotted lines in Figure 3 indicate the holding stitches on the face of the embroidery.

This method of attaching a strip of material to a background results in a smoother line of pattern than the other similar techniques. Only faint lines where the edges of the strips show are apparent in this smooth band. Usually strips of thin material create fainter lines than strips that are thicker. The width of the pattern created with this and other similar techniques does not have to remain the same dimension. It can be adjusted so it will narrow or widen gradually to conform to a pattern with curved lines, especially if the strip of material that is attached has some elasticity. Leather strips cut from the fine, soft, thin leather of women's dress gloves usually have this elasticity. In some of the motifs of Photo 4, continuous leather pattern bands of equal width within a motif were used. Where the two sides meet in a point, in some motifs the pattern bands were narrowed to form these points. Strips from very thin material are needed to form sharp points.

At the top of Photo 5, two of the four samples of this technique show variations that can be introduced into the attached bands just described. The two upper strips were cut from pellon. The left sample of the next line was made from a sheer ribbon and decorated with additional diagonal stitches of embroidery thread. The right sample of this line was made with a heavy felted material and stitched in a horizontal line through the middle of the band, also with embroidery thread.

There is one variation of this technique in which the width of the patterned band remains constant. The strips that are fastened at the lower and upper edges of the pattern are attached as shown in Figures 1 and 2. Horizontal strips are added to the band, and the number used is governed by their width and the width of the pattern band. The strips can be narrower, wider, or the same width as the vertical ones, and they can contrast in color, in texture, or both. As the vertical strips pass from the top to the bottom only, they are interwoven with the horizontal strips; therefore, the horizontal strips are positioned over the vertical strips that pass from the bottom to the top. Three horizontal strips about the same width as the vertical strips are interwoven in Figure 4.

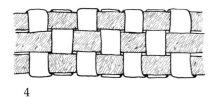

4

Photo 3. Grosgrain ribbon applied to a denim background using quillwork and couching techniques. *Photographer, Harold Tacker.*

Photo 5. Porcupine quill embroidery techniques are executed in ribbons and cut strips of fabric on this sampler. *Photographer, William Eng.*

Photo 4. Quillwork using leather strips combined with traditional embroidery makes handsome motifs on the black background fabric of this unfinished panel. *Photographer, Harold Tacker.*

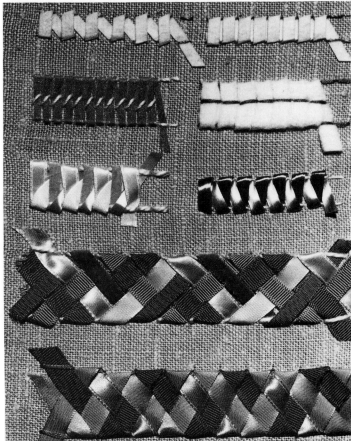

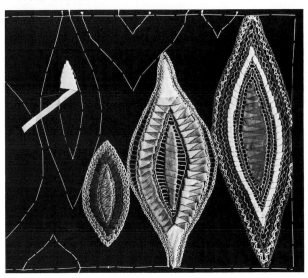

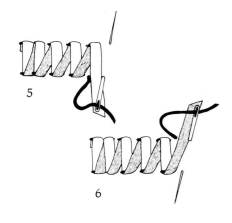

5

6

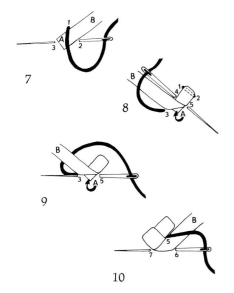

7

8

9

10

Other variations of the bands created as shown in Figures 1 and 2 give different effects. The stitching on these variations is along the top and bottom of the pattern band, but the strips that are applied to the background are folded in a different way. In Photo 5, the right-hand sample of the third row from the top is made with a ribbon that is one color on the face and another color on the reverse. This same effect can be achieved by using two lightweight ribbons of different colors placed back to back and treated as one.

The method for stitching these strips is a little easier to execute than the method that was previously described. As shown in Figures 5 and 6, the strip is always laid in place, stitched and then folded over the holding stitch after it is completed. This is easier than the first technique explained because in it the strip is folded and then the stitch is completed, so it is necessary to adjust the fold as the stitch is tightened.

In Photo 5, the left sample in the third row and the two lower samples are made with multiple colors or textures of ribbons held at the edges of the bands in the same manner illustrated in Figures 5 and 6. The sample in the third row is made with two different ribbons, the one below it is made with four ribbons that are interwoven as they pass from the top to the bottom of the band, and the bottom one is made with three ribbons interwoven in a different pattern. In the lower sample, each ribbon is interwoven as it crosses another ribbon. In the sample above it, some of the ribbons float over other ribbons as they cross them, instead of interweaving with each one.

The technique used for the solidly covered parts of Photo 3 also attaches the strip to the background under the folds, but it is folded first to the right, then to the left to make a zigzag line of pattern. The strip A-B in Figure 7 is laid on the background diagonally so A is at the lower left and B is at the upper right, then A is stitched across near the end. The needle comes up at 1 on the upper left side of the strip, and it goes down at 2 on the lower right side. The end B folds over this stitch, so the stitch is pulled as firmly as possible without puckering either the strip or the background. In Figure 8, end B has been folded over and hides all but a little of the A end under it, then B is folded again, this time diagonally, so it turns to the left and forms a right angle to the section on the right. The stitching thread has come out at 3 and it goes back into the background at 4, thus fastening B down so it can be folded again. (If a slippery material is used for the strip, an additional stitch, as shown in Figure 9, can be used to hold it firmly. First stitch up through the background at 3 and down at 5 with the stitching thread going under the B section of the strip, and then stitch from 3 to 4 as shown in Figure 8.) To continue, B is folded over the 3-4 stitch covering both the end A and the previous diagonal fold (Fig. 10). Again, B is folded diagonally and at a right angle to itself and fastened by inserting the needle into the background at 6 and coming out at 7 to prepare for the next stitch. For slippery material, another stitch similar to the one shown in Figure 9 is placed between 5 and 7 before end B is folded over the 5-6 holding stitch. The 5-6 stitch is a repeat of the 1-2 stitch, so the work continues with the steps given in Figures 7, 9 if necessary, 8, and 10.

If these zigzag lines are folded and stitched carefully, as in Photo 3, they can be fitted together to make solid areas of pattern with no background showing except at the edges. In Photo 3, starting at the bottom, an olive green row is followed by a turquoise one fitted into the first row. Then the background is allowed to show in squares between this and the next row by placing these two rows point to point instead of fitting one into another. The third row is purple, followed by light green and turquoise, and then olive green outlines the rectangle on the left. The third, fourth, fifth, and sixth rows are fitted together so no background shows between them. The rectangle is bordered, first by the olive green row just mentioned; then reading from the outside row inward, the next row is a light blue row placed point to point with the olive green row, and then a purple row. Light green is used for the base of the couched motifs, and they are couched with olive green and turquoise braids. The turquoise braid is held in place with olive green embroidery thread, and the olive green braid is couched with turquoise embroidery thread. The piece will be lined, then mounted to be used as a small wall hanging.

A less angular version of the technique just described can be made by using a softer material for the strip, and starting the work from the part of the design nearest you and working away from instead of toward you. A holding stitch is placed across the end of the strip, as shown in Figure 11. The short end of the strip faces away from you, and this time it can be puckered by the holding stitch if desired. This is true of the holding stitches for the entire length this technique is worked.

The needle is brought through the background at 1 and down at 2 for the stitch that holds the end in place, then it is brought back through the background at 3 to begin the next holding stitch (Fig. 12). Before the 3-4 holding stitch is completed, the strip is folded at approximately 3-4 and brought downward and to the left. The needle is passed under the fold and down through 4, thus holding this fold in place when the stitch is tightened. When the needle goes through the background at 4, it comes back to the surface at 5, which is below and to the left of 3. This stitch (Fig. 13) is completed by going into the background at 6 and out again at 7. As soon as this is tightened, the strip is folded upward over itself, as shown in Figure 14. The 7-8 holding stitch is completed by coming up through the background at 9. The 9-10 stitch is the same as the 1-2 stitch, so the sequence is repeated to continue. See Figure 15 for the stitch sequence, and the lower band in Photo 6 for the appearance of a pattern made with grosgrain ribbon using this technique. Photo 7 shows three rows of the design worked with rayon braid in turquoise and white. They are fitted together to form a solid surface.

For a right-handed person, the upper band in Photo 6 is worked more easily from right to left, as shown in Figure 16. In this diagram the starting end of the strip has been fastened in place with a stitch. If it is desirable to hide this first stitch, as well as the beginning end of the strip, the visible parts should be tucked back and stitched where the strip will cover them when it is folded over. The appearance of this band is similar to the one diagrammed in Figures 1 and 2; however, this technique is usually used for narrower bands made with strips of material that has some stiffness. The material should bend easily without breaking, yet it must be stiff enough to hold the strips in place without being stitched at each fold.

The right side of Figure 16 illustrates the contiguous relationship among the first three units of the worked band. All units of a band worked in this technique should be spaced this way. The third and fourth sections of this diagram are separated to show how the stitch holds the strip in place. When all of the sections of this band are laid next to each other, the stitching is hidden under the band, and the stitches are closer together than shown in Figure 16. Also the position of the needle will be more nearly vertical as each stitch is taken. Several rows of this technique, fitted together to make a solid surface, are shown in Photo 8.

An adjustment in this technique, not found in porcupine quill embroidery,

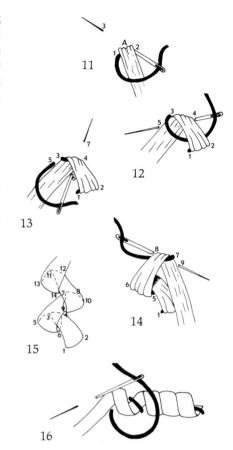

Photo 6. Three quillwork techniques worked with ribbons. *Photographer, William Eng.*

Photo 7. Three rows of blue and white narrow braid were stitched in quillwork techniques so they fit together to make a solid pattern area on a ground of red material quilted in squares. *Photographer, Harold Tacker.*

Photo 8. Six bands of a quillwork technique made with blue and white narrow braids create a solid surface on a red background. *Photographer, Harold Tacker.*

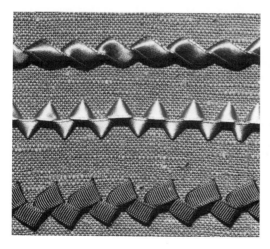
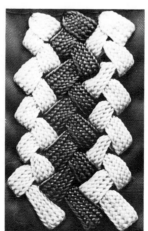

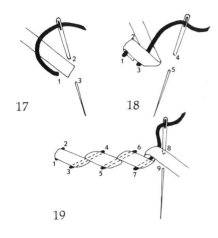

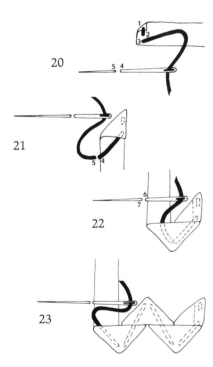

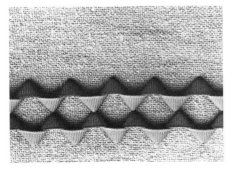

Photo 9. Two rows of blue grosgrain ribbon worked in a quillwork technique on a tan fabric background. *Photographer, Harold Tacker.*

can be made for a softer material such as the satin ribbon shown in the top row of Photo 6. The band has a different appearance because each section is positioned at a greater angle than in the previously explained band. Also, the band can be worked from right to left, and longer stitches hold the two folds and the strip more firmly. The strip is laid on the background, almost in a vertical position, with one end placed on the background where the work will begin. The strip will extend slightly upward and to the left, as in Figure 17. The end of the strip is fastened to the background with stitch 1-2, and the needle emerges at 3. In Figure 18, the strip is folded over the 1-2 stitch, brought downward, and then folded upward so the left edge of the fold is next to 3; the strip folds under itself going upward so the left edge passes by where the needle went into the background at 2. The holding stitch passes between the two parts of the strip that make the fold and extends far enough beyond the strip to allow a second fold in the strip, as shown in Figure 19. Actually, the strip wraps around the stitch, and it is adjusted so it fits firmly as the stitch is tightened to hold it in place.

The last technique to be described here is another method of stitching a strip on a background. This technique makes a band of pattern that resembles rickrack, and it too can be stitched so the rows fit together to make a solid surface. The middle row of Photo 6 shows a single row of this technique made with satin ribbon.

To begin a row of this technique, lay a strip in a horizontal position on a background, as shown in Figure 20. At the left end of the horizontal strip, turn the upper corner down so it makes a triangle on top of the strip, bring the needle up from the reverse side of the background at 1 so it penetrates the strip and the corner of it that has been turned down. Stitch down at 2 and back up again at 3, thus attaching the end of the strip to the background. Fold the strip over these stitches so the long end is at the left. Fold this end again, this time diagonally and under itself so the long end is downward as in Figure 21. Figure 20 shows the needle stitching at 4-5; however, the two folds should be made before the short 4-5 stitch is taken because the stitching thread must be on top of the strip after it is folded, as shown in Figure 21. As soon as stitch 4-5 is taken, the strip is folded diagonally again, this time over itself with the end extended to the left (Fig. 22). Then turn the strip under itself with another diagonal fold so the end of it extends upward. When the strip extends upward, take stitch 6-7, another short stitch. The upper triangle that follows is folded in the same sequence as the lower one, first over itself so the end of the strip extends to the left, then under itself (Fig. 23) so the strip points downward. These two triangles are stitched to the background alternately to form a row of this quillwork technique. Photo 9 shows two rows of this technique worked point to point so squares of background are formed between them.

Quillwork can be seen in many displays of Indian artifacts, and William C. Orchard gives many other quillwork techniques in his article listed in the bibliography. After working some of the techniques given here, then inspecting some of the quillwork in museums, you will have a greater respect for the painstaking work produced by the Indian women, particularly when you remember they stitched with an awl and sinew, and their strips came in very short lengths. Quillwork techniques worked in ribbon and other materials can produce dramatic embroideries quickly, but the work done with porcupine quills, especially the finer ones which took time, care and patience, deserves the greatest respect.

BIBLIOGRAPHY

Feder, Norman. *Art of the Eastern Plains Indians, The Nathan Sturges Jarvis Collection.* New York: The Brooklyn Museum. 1934.

Lyford, Carrie A. *Quill and Beadwork of the Western Sioux.* United States Department of the Interior, Bureau of Indian Affairs, Department of Education. 1940.

Odle, Robin. "Quill and Moosehair Work in the Great Lakes Region." In *Arts of the Great Lakes Indians.* Flint, Michigan: Flint Institute of the Arts, 1973.

Orchard, William C. *The Techniques of Porcupine Quill Decoration Among the North American Indians.* New York: The Museum of the American Indian (Heye Foundation), Vol. IV, No. 1. 1916.

I first met Anne Blinks 30 years ago, in the early '50's, in Washington, D.C. The Blinkses were residing temporarily in Washington, and Anne came to the Textile Museum to find something to occupy her time. I was then a young Museum Assistant. Irene Emery, who had only recently been hired as Curator of Technical Studies, immediately seized upon Anne's offer of her time and skills and set her to weaving examples of fabric structures. Irene's "samples" were all woven with the same weight and ply of white string (although I seem to recall a problem in getting what she wanted) and to the same size. They were then painstakingly lit and photographed to provide the illustrations for her Primary Structures of Fabrics (1966). I have no idea how many of the illustrations were woven by Irene herself and how many by Anne, but I do remember Anne toiling over the loom in what was then the museum library.

Anne was always fascinated by odd techniques, and I also remember her struggles with a vantsöm mitten and her interest in sprang. Irene shared her interests, which led to many lively technical discussions. In the "acknowledgements" portion of Primary Structures, Irene gave "Special thanks . . . to Mrs. Anne Blinks, who took an enthusiastic and active part in several aspects of the investigation. . . ." (1966:xiv). Sprang was something that interested all of us, and later, when I was working on my dissertation, Textiles and Basketry of the Paracas Period, Ica Valley, Peru (1965), we set up a sprang frame, of sorts, in Irene's office. Some of the Peruvian sprang, notably that from Nazca, is extremely complicated, being double oblique twining! In my spare time, I would play with the sprang frame, trying to achieve this wonder. One day I succeeded! The only problem was that I didn't know how I had done it, and I could never do it again. Fortunately, Peter Collingwood (1974:202ff and Pl.43) has since worked it out and gives detailed instructions.

This article, then, is for Anne, on her 80th birthday, with love and admiration.

Portions of this article are abstracted from my dissertation (King, 1965).

SPRANG IN THE PARACAS PERIOD OF PERU

BY MARY ELIZABETH KING

Sprang is a fabric consisting of a single set of elements. In the manufacturing process, these elements are fixed at both ends to a frame. In his work, *The Techniques of Sprang*, Peter Collingwood (1974:31) notes, "As an inevitable result of the warp being fixed at both ends, corresponding but contrary movements of the threads appear simultaneously at its other end." Sprang can also be done on a circular warp. Working from the center, the fabric builds from both ends toward the middle. While the work is in progress, the elements are held in place by a series of sticks. The fabric produced is often lace-like openwork, but it can also be compact and braid-like. A characteristic of sprang is the finish line or "meeting" line which usually consists of a chained row at the center designed to hold the elements in place. Occasionally, the fabric is cut at this point and knotted.

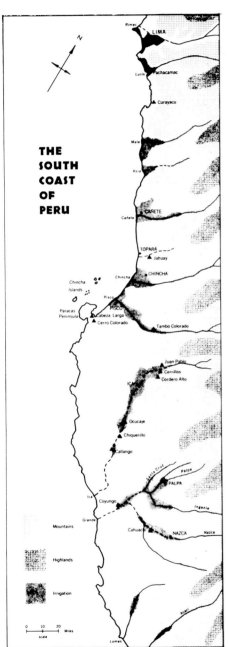

Figure 1. The South Coast of Peru, showing location of sites. (after Sawyer, 1966).

The word, sprang, is Scandinavian. According to Collingwood (1973:34), *sprangning* ". . . originally meant any openwork textile." *Sprang* is now used, in Scandinavia, to refer to the processes Emery (1966:69) calls "frame interlinking", "oblique frame interlacing", and "oblique frame twining". It tends also to be used in English for the fabric itself, for which the correct term would be *sprangning*.

I will use sprang as a collective term for these frame-made structures and use Emery's terms for the individual techniques.

In any case, sprang, especially the form Emery calls frame interlinking, appears to have a long known history, with a series of dates in the first millennium B.C. in both the Old and New Worlds. Unfortunately, unless the "meeting" or finish line is present, sprang cannot be distinguished from ordinary interlinking, oblique interlacing (braiding or plaiting), or oblique twining. Interlinking and oblique interlacing both appear very early in most areas, but they certainly cannot be definitely said to be sprang. The origins of sprang are, of course, lost to us. Since textiles are so very perishable, it is unlikely that we will find many examples earlier than those we now have dating from about 8000 B.C. in both Old and New Worlds. In neither case is sprang one of these earliest known techniques.

Since a frame is necessary for the production of sprang, it probably cannot be counted among the earliest techniques known to man. These are almost certainly those that require no tools or apparatus other than human hands and perhaps something, such as a tree or bush, to which to tie a suspension cord. Once the concept of a knotted cord was mastered, the way was paved for more complicated structures. The single element techniques—linking, looping, and knotted netting—must almost certainly be the earliest, perhaps together with those techniques made with a single set of elements, such as interlinking, oblique interlacing and oblique twining. Although the case cannot, of course, be proven, two-single-element constructions, such as looping and linking on foundation cords, may precede the two-sets-of-interactive element techniques such as twining. Once a frame is required, sprang would easily proceed from known set-of-element techniques. Thus one might expect it to follow closely on the advent of twining.

The earliest known examples of interlinking definitely made on a frame are from the Danish Bronze age (ca. 1400 B.C.) and consist of a cap and a hairnet. There are also European Iron Age examples, and later, Coptic examples from Egypt. Most, if not all, of these early pieces are hairnets, caps or bags. More recent historic European examples also include stockings, mittens, collars, cuffs, belts and sashes, garters, carrying bands, borders, and even skirts and jackets (Collingwood 1974:37ff).

In the New World, the earliest certain examples of sprang are from the Middle Paracas period (ca. 200-100 B.C.) of the South Coast of Peru. Engel (1963:38) has claimed to have examples of sprang from the late Preceramic Central Coast site of Asia (ca. 1100 B.C.) in Peru. He does not, however, seem to understand the technique, and some of his technical identifications are highly dubious. He states that cylindrical bags, with a starting point in the bottom center, are sprang, though they are probably cross-knit looping. One example has an interlinked rim. Other pieces (for example, Engel, 1963: Figs. 64, 65, 87) could be sprang, but neither in his illustrations nor descriptions is a finish line indicated. His description of sprang is as follows: "In loom-plaiting, sets of yarns are plaited together according to the desired pattern" (Engel, 1963:38).

Wallace (1962 and 1982 personal communications) found one example of sprang at the South Coast site of Cerillos, not in his earliest levels, but in the La Isla (ca. 500-300 B.C.), or early Paracas, level. This may be the earliest known example in the New World. It has a simple geometric design in interlinking. The center finish line is present.

Although it is possible that the use of sprang dates to the Preceramic period, it might also have arisen in the Chavin period from a base of Preceramic interlinking.

Examination of Engel's materials by a textile specialist should prove the point.

Sprang has been well known from Paracas since the early 1930's. O'Neale(1937:197 and 1942:161-162) described two "headdresses" from Paracas Caverns as "twined" and of "orange wool". She did not illustrate these headdresses in full, but she included sketches of the design of one, interlocking snakes and fish motifs (MN 8430; Fig. 11), and of the technique (MN 8430; Fig. 10). They are clearly of oblique interlinking rather than twining. D'Harcourt also illustrates MN 8430 (1962:Pl. b) and describes it as ". . . plaited of brown wool in accordance with the technique by which the yarns are fastened at their ends and twisted together" (1962:161). I have notes on a sprang fragment in the collections of the Museo Nacional de Antropología in Lima (MNAA 13/152), which is of gold-tan wool, but it was too fragmentary to determine its shape or function. It was also, however, from the Paracas Caverns.

The original site of Paracas, from which the above pieces came, is located on the neck of the Paracas Peninsula, on the South Coast of Peru (Fig. 1). Julio C. Tello, who began to excavate the site in 1925, found two types of graves. On the basis of these, he established a Paracas culture, which he divided into Paracas Cavernas and Paracas Necropolis. The former produced a wide variety of techniques, while the latter is known chiefly for its elaborately embroidered garments. The textiles were found wrapped around seated bodies in "mummy bundles".

There is a time difference between these two Paracas phases. Cavernas is now considered to be Middle Paracas (ca. 200 B.C.-100 B.C., or Ocucaje 9); while Necropolis is late Paracas (ca. 100 B.C.-A.D. 1, or Ocucaje 10 and Nazca 1). Other Paracas phases and sites have since been identified. One of them, the site of Ocucaje, on the Hacienda Ocucaje about 25 km south of the city of Ica, was first visited by Max Uhle in 1901 (Uhle, 1914).

Although Ocucaje has produced materials from a longer time range than the site of Paracas itself, the bulk of the textiles from Ocucaje appear to be closely related to those from Cavernas.

The textiles that are discussed in this paper are from a collection purchased jointly by the Textile Museum of Washington, D.C., and the American Museum of Natural History, New York City, in 1957. The total collection contains about 700 artifacts and includes some 250 textiles or textile fragments.

The Ocucaje collection contains four examples of sprang. Two are "hoods" (TM 91.895 and AMNH 41.2/5982), rectangular pieces of sprang folded along the central chain line and sewn along one long side and across the end (Fig. 2). A third fragment (TM 91.867) may also be from a hood. The fourth example (AMNH 41.2/6164) appears to be a fragment of a bag.

The "hoods", which are presumably what O'Neale called "headdresses", are a type of garment not previously reported from Peru. Since they resemble nothing so much as a shallow bag or pillowcase, one would not ordinarily associate them with something worn on the head. However, Pablo Soldi, who assembled the collection, reported that they were sometimes found over the heads and hanging down the backs of mummies, and they are shown being worn on some figurines.

In addition to the sprang examples, there are also two double-cloth hoods (TM 91.873 and 91.877) which match a double-cloth mantle (TM 91.872) and constitute the only known matching garments from Ocucaje.

The two sprang hoods each have a row of multicolored fringe sewn around the open edges. Two of the hoods are of wool; the fragmentary one is of cotton. Two (one wool and the other cotton) have interlocking snake motifs; the third has an elaborate design of cat-headed figures (Photos 1 and 2).

Although the figurine suggests otherwise, it is possible that these hoods were meant only for burial and were never worn in life.

The fourth sprang fragment (AMNH 41.2/6164) is also of considerable interest. It appears to be a bag fragment (Photo 3); and it contained a second, smaller bag (?) of plaid plain weave. Unfortunately, the finish line is missing

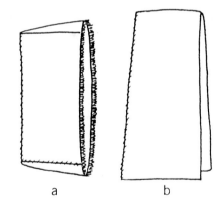

a   b

Figure 2. Diagram of the construction of the Paracas "hoods". a. Sprang type; b. double-cloth type.

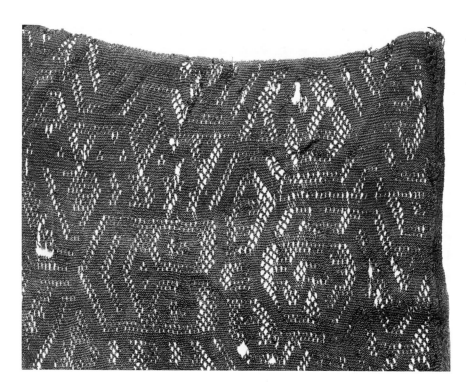

Photo 1. Detail of a sprang hood (TM 91.895). *Photograph courtesy of The Textile Museum, Washington, D.C.*

Photo 2. A complete sprang hood from Ocucaje, Textile Museum 91.895, with an elaborate cat-headed figure motif. *Photograph courtesy of the Textile Museum, Washington, D.C.*

Photo 3. Sprang bag fragment from Ocucaje, American Museum of Natural History 41.2/6164. *Photograph courtesy of the American Museum of Natural History, New York.*

on this piece; however, it is unlikely that it was made by any other method than sprang.

This fragment appears to have a geometric design, probably simple open rectangles. The most interesting thing about this bag is that it has a narrow slit tapestry border with zigzag lines of cream and green on a black ground. A wider tapestry fragment, also with sprang attached, which cannot be joined to the bag in any meaningful way now, has a guilloche motif in red, cream, and green on a black ground. Tapestry is extremely rare from Paracas.

All of the known Paracas sprang is relatively simple oblique interlinking (Fig. 3). The designs, however, range from simple to complex. Although we cannot be sure what device was used to string the warps, Johnson (1958:206) reports that in modern Mexican and Guatemalan sprang production, the back-strap loom is often used as the frame. We may presume that the same was true in preconquest Peru.

It is clear that the technique had been totally mastered by the Paracas period. Thus one might expect to find still earlier examples of sprang, from the Chavin period and, perhaps, from the Preceramic period. By the Nazca period (ca. A.D. 1-A.D. 500), which follows the Paracas period, sprang had been developed to incredible lengths. The typical Nazca sprang examples (Photo 4) are curious bell-shaped "tassels", which d'Harcourt (1962:81-82, 161, and Pls. 57, 58) called "neck coverings". D'Harcourt correctly described them as "loom plaiting", but did not diagram them. These tassels (and we still do not know exactly how they were used) occur in pairs attached to a very narrow, long band. They are always double "cloth" and sometimes have four interchanged colors (in two layers). When they are completed, they are folded in half, and the finish line is covered with embroidery. The technique is double oblique twining (see Collingwood, 1974:202, Fig. 111, [b]). Collingwood (1974:202) indicates that oblique ". . . intertwining is the least used of the thread structures produced by the sprang method; in fact it is only recorded (historically) from Peru." It has, however, been reported ethnologically among the Guajiro in Colombia, who use it for hammocks (Collingwood, 1974:202).

It is a technique that inspires admiration for its makers. D'Harcourt (1962:81) remarks that the construction of these pieces ". . . presupposes the complete mastery of a technique that is in this case particularly complex." Collingwood (1974:217-218) says of double oblique twined sprang:

Figure 3. Diagram of the oblique interlinking form of sprang used in Paracas hoods.

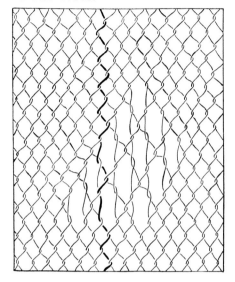

Photo 4. A Nazca sprang tassel of double, oblique twining, Textile Museum 1959.11.3. *Photograph courtesy of the Textile Museum, Washington, D.C.*

The Peruvian examples use a variant of intertwining which is difficult to analyse. They were very advanced technically and often included areas of interlacing at the beginning and end of the fabric and of interlinking between vertical color boundaries. . . . Examples exist in which two double intertwined sprang fabrics were worked one in front of the other. At various levels, the threads of the two double fabrics changed places completely. So what was, say, a red and black fabric with, say, a green and blue fabric behind it, became a green and blue fabric with a red and black fabric behind it. These are probably the most complex sprang fabrics ever produced.

The production of such an incredibly complex fabric, for what seems to us a relatively unimportant article of clothing, is very like the ancient Peruvians, who seem to have reveled in experimentation of the most involved sort.

Sprang is earlier in Peru than in any other part of the New World, but this may be due simply to accidents of preservation. The technique is known in Mexico and Guatemala today (see Johnson, 1958) and may well have been present prehistorically. It occurs relatively late in the prehistory of the Southwestern United States and persists in the form of Hopi wedding sashes (see Kent, 1957:603-605).

If, indeed, the technique is eventually found in early Preceramic period sites in Peru, it would suggest that it was one of the techniques brought with the early migrants from Asia. On the other hand, the apparent absence of the technique from that part of the world suggests even more strongly that sprang was independently invented in Europe or Africa and in Peru.

REFERENCES CITED

Collingwood, Peter. *The Techniques of Sprang: Plaiting on Stretched Threads.* New York: Watson-Guptill Publications, 1974.

Emery, Irene. *The Primary Structures of Fabrics: An Illustrated Classification.* Washington, D.C.: The Textile Museum, 1966.

Engel, Frederic. "A Preceramic Settlement on the Central Coast of Peru: Asia, Unit 1". *Transactions of the American Philosophical Society,* Vol. 53, Part 3, 1963.

Harcourt, Raoul d'. *Textiles of Ancient Peru and Their Techniques.* Seattle: University of Washington Press, 1962.

Johnson, Irmgard. "Twine-Plaiting in the New World". *Proceedings of the 32nd International Congress of Americanists,* pp. 198-213. Copenhagen: 1958.

Kent, Kate Peck. "The Cultivation and Weaving of Cotton in the Prehistoric Southwestern United States". *Transactions of the American Philosophical Society,* Vol. 47, Part 3, 1957.

King, Mary Elizabeth. *Textiles and Basketry of the Paracas Period, Ica Valley, Peru.* Ph.D. Dissertation, The University of Arizona, Tucson, 1965.

O'Neale, Lila M. Tejidos del periodo primitivo de Paracas. In "Una exploracion en Cerro Colorado", by E. Yacovleff and J.C. Muelle, pp. 60-80. *Revista del Museo Nacional,* Vol. 1, No. 2, pp. 31-102. Lima, Peru: 1932.

-----. "Archaeological Explorations in Peru. Part III, Textiles of the Early Nazca Period". *Field Museum of Natural History, Anthropology, Memoirs,* Vol. 2, No. 3, 1937.

-----. "Textile Periods in Ancient Peru: II, Paracas Caverns and the Grand Necropolis". *University of California Publications in American Archaeology and Ethnology,* Vol. 39, No. 2, 1942, pp. 143-202. Berkeley, California: 1942.

Sawyer, Alan. *Ancient Peruvian Ceramics: The Nathan Cummings Collection.* New York: The Metropolitan Museum of Art, 1966.

Uhle, Max. "The Nazca Pottery of Ancient Peru". *Proceedings of the Davenport Academy of Sciences,* Vol. 13, 1914, pp. 1-16. Davenport, Iowa: 1914.

Photo 1. Narrow band in saha weave from Afghanistan, revealing the floats on the reverse side. *Photography, Terry Gritton.*

THE BEDOUIN SAHA WEAVE AND ITS DOUBLE CLOTH COUSIN

BY MARTHA STANLEY

On the simplest of ground looms in parts of the Middle East two notably different yet remarkably related textiles are woven, the saha tent curtain and its structural offspring, the Sudanese camel girth.

The English woman Grace Crowfoot wrote the primary description of them as a result of her travels and years of living and observing weaving in the Middle East. Her descriptions are charming, sensitive, detailed. Listed in the bibliography, they are well worth tracking down and reading. Anne Blinks became greatly interested in Grace Crowfoot and her writings in the 1950's. Early in 1957 Anne sailed to England to study with her. Crowfoot's untimely death forced Anne to turn to the British Museum where she abstracted numerous Crowfoot papers. In 1973, when I expressed interest in trying to weave saha from a description in Peter Collingwood's *The Techniques of Rug Weaving* (pp. 449-451), Anne came forth immediately. She generously shared her findings at the British Museum, and we both wove one-weft double cloth "sahas" on a rugged old Swedish loom of hers.

It is these two weaves, the warp pattern plain weave of the saha curtain and the one-weft double cloth of the camel girth, which shall be discussed here. The descriptions are not based upon my personal observations of the Bedouin, but stem from close reading of Crowfoot's careful observations and my own efforts on ground and floor looms.

The saha cloth is woven by Bedouin women in black and white and occasional red, of goat hair and cotton, on primitive ground looms. It hangs inside their tents, which they have also woven of black goat hair. This saha curtain plays a special role for the women. Its weaving permits the creative expression of their design forms. Hung horizontally as the dividing curtain in the tent, it perpetuates the social divisions between men and women. It defines the tent space occupied by the man, his fire for preparing coffee for his guests, and the guests themselves. On the other side of this dividing curtain are the women, children, foodstuffs, and occasional animals. The saha's function is not so much to isolate as to demarcate. Hanging clear to the floor, its top edge is around shoulder height. One can easily peek or peer over it when standing to get a glimpse of what is being overheard on the other side.

The camel girth is just that—a sturdy, narrow band for cinching saddles and caravan litters onto Bedouin camels. The girth has handsome patterns woven into its strength, reflecting the important position the camel has in their lives. In a way of life with relatively few personal possessions, beauty is wed to the most useful, most important. In a landscape where beauty is as sparse as water, there is a thirst for the decorative.

We begin by looking at the two textiles, front and back. The warp patterned saha weave is all warp face plain weave on the front surface in two colors. Each thread either weaves on the surface or floats on the reverse side until the design calls it back to the woven surface again. Thus the woven side of the cloth has all points of interlacement represented on the surface by a thread of either one color or the other in a dense warp face plain weave, articulate and beautiful in pattern, firm in structure. The woven surface exhibits the tightly spun, smooth lozenge shape presented by each thread. The clear design lines on the front, of converging horizontal and diagonal color changes, become bloated, indistinct, and animated on the reverse — much as on the reverse side of a woven label in an article of our clothing.

In the Sudan the camel girths are woven on similar looms. In a narrower width, these girths have a similarly tight plain weave pattern on one side. The other side is identical to the front but with the colors reversing roles in the design. Closer examination reveals a one-weft double cloth flattened tube with the two layers interlocked at the edges and at all points where the colors change in a horizontal or diagonal plane in the cloth.

In both textiles the clearest color demarcations occur along diagonal lines, reflecting color change, not diagonal movement, of warps. Designs abound in triangles, diamonds, zigzags, stepped diagonals. The striking beauty is matched by the great simplicity of the plain weave warp setup.

Each weave is accomplished on a very simple ground loom consisting of two pieces of wood staked apart on the ground to form warp beams, with one heddle rod, propped permanently up on stones at either side of the warp, and a shed rod which moves up close behind the heddles, giving access to the counter shed. That such a primitive loom can produce as lovely and well woven a cloth as the saha seems a fine tribute to the weaving skills of Bedouin women. But that this same loom produces a double cloth is staggering to contemporary floor loom weavers. After all, one learns early on in our weaving circles that it takes a minimum of four harnesses to weave double cloth! Let us examine how each of these weaves is executed and all will become clearer, yet probably no less magical.

First we look at the saha since it is the simpler of the two structures. A warp is made of the desired length using two balls, one of each color in the pattern. The Bedouin woman passes a loop from each ball simultaneously around the end of one warp beam and then around the other in figure eight fashion. The figure eight passage of the balls, of course, maintains the order of the threads. Since both threads travel the same path together, the figure eight cross is comprised of alternating pairs, each having a light and a dark thread. Throughout the processes of warping and making the sheds, the integrity of this duet of threads is maintained. If two women warp together, the heddling may be done by one of them as the warp is wound. Otherwise it is done after warping is completed. In either case, every other pair is heddled, with alternate pairs passing on top of a shed rod. Thus we find a light-dark pair in the same heddle and the next pair over the shed rod. In warping and preparing the sheds, the Bedouin woman has also created her loom.

After the warp has been readied, a stick is wound with weft and the weaving commences. A sword is put in the first shed to isolate the top layer's myriad of threads (heddle rod's shed) from those in the bottom. Through each heddle pass both a light and a dark warp. According to her chosen design, the weaver selects the warp thread of the proper color and holds it in reserve on her arm or a pick-up stick — often a gazelle horn. She drops its unwanted mate which falls below to rest on the sword. When each pair of threads has been sorted so that one warp from each heddle has been chosen and its complement dropped, she inserts the weft and changes the shed.

Because this weave is warp face, the weft is almost completely covered. With only one thread of each pair appearing on the woven surface, it can be readily imagined that this warp is quite dense. Changing sheds is a tiresome and arduous process. The shed rod is brought forward directly behind the heddles. A small segment of warps is raised slightly, directly over the shed rod. A few at a time these warps are "snapped" through the layer of heddled threads, to appear now as the new shed. The weaver carefully works her way across the warp, transposing the two layers of threads. Once again she enters the sword to maintain the shed separation and beat down the weft firmly.

Photo 2. Author's ground loom. Design of the cloth is not Bedouin.

A suitably curved gazelle horn aids in this beating operation. She slips the tool under small groups of warps of the new top shed and thwacks the weft down firmly against the cloth. Pick-up is now done on this new shed: selecting the desired color, dropping the unwanted one, entering the weft. Then she moves the shed rod back away from the heddle rod. Close to the heddles she pushes the warp down, somewhat as a kitten kneads while nursing. Downward pressure on the tensioned warp forces the shed rod threads below the permanently-elevated heddled warps. The heddle rod shed has returned to the top layer; the sword is reinserted.

And so the weaving continues. The fingers dextrously select and drop warps. The hands and eyes check whether all the appropriate threads have been isolated. The process repeats itself pick after pick under the skill of the weaver. The design advances slowly and steadily into the sea of warp threads. Underneath, the discarded warps float in bloated negative imagery of the front. When the cloth has advanced sufficiently toward the heddles so that more working space is required for pick-up, the shed rod is pushed further back. The heddle rod is taken down from its perch on the stones, they are moved further back and the rod repositioned. As the stretch becomes too great for the weaver, she moves to the other side of the breast beam and sits on her woven efforts as she continues. The cloth becomes her rug as she weaves.

Having seen how the saha is woven, we turn now to the second textile. The remarkable feature of the camel girth is that its transformed (tamed, if you will) double cloth reverse side is so simple to achieve. The front side is woven identically to that of the saha. Then the discarded threads of the pick-up are captured almost magically with remarkably little additional effort. To get the top layer requires pick-up. The bottom layer can be isolated and woven without resort to additional pick-up. First let us examine how this is accomplished; we can then probe its mysteries and marvel at so simple a solution.

As in the warp patterned saha, the top threads of the shed are isolated with a camel rib sword and pick-up is worked. The weft is inserted and beaten down to the fell of the cloth with this camel rib sword, weaving the top surface. The rib, however, is NOT removed; it is also brought down to the fell of the cloth and remains in the shed. Now the shed is changed to bring to the surface all the alternate shed's warps. Another camel rib sword is put in this new shed. Both sticks are now turned on edge, producing an exaggeration of the cross created by the new shed and the picked-up top layer. Underneath this cross is revealed an additional, triangularly-shaped space with only the discarded warps from the pick-up forming its bottom. The weft is now inserted in this "X" shed and returns to the edge of the cloth it originated from. The pick-up stick in the top layer is removed and the shed change previously executed is now beaten clear down to the fell of the cloth. Both layers of the

Photo 3. Getting the "X" shed.

first pick of double cloth have been woven, and the weaver is ready to begin the pick-up on the new shed.

Most picked-up double cloths require pick-up for the bottom layer as well as the top. The camel girth — to use an old cliché — gives two for the price of one. It really seems quite amazing that with so few additional movements the weaver gains a second woven layer — and a reversible fabric. Because these additional movements seem so unrelated to pick-up, the result is puzzling also. An explanation may clarify the process.

This is a densely warp-faced weave with the weft essentially invisible. As such it does not require two wefts matching the colors of each pattern segment to achieve a pure rendering of the color of one design area, but is woven as a one-weft double cloth. This single weft's passage is directly across in the top layer, returning to the starting edge in the bottom, so that a flattened tube is formed. (In a balanced plain weave double cloth in which the weft were visible on the surfaces of both layers, a black weft would be necessary in the black design areas and a white in the white areas. Thus when the black warps appeared in the top layer, the black weft would weave there. When the black warps dove to the bottom layer, their matching weft would follow. The white weft's path would be directly opposite and complementary to the black's. This dipping of the wefts from top to bottom shed and back would require pick-up to isolate the correct path for each of the two wefts, twice as much pick-up as in the camel girth.)

When the weft's passage is so direct, the correct threads for the bottom layer may be isolated with simple shed manipulation. Let us re-examine the weaving process to understand this fully. When the first shed is opened, one-half of the total warp threads are raised. In the act of pick-up, half of the threads of this shed are dropped and a camel rib sword inserted so that the chosen threads are above it, the discards below. After weft insertion, the camel rib sword remains in the top layer's shed. The shed is changed, and the second rib inserted in the new shed. The entire set of warps of the opposite shed floats over this rib. An inventory of all the threads passing by these two ribs is given in Figure 1.

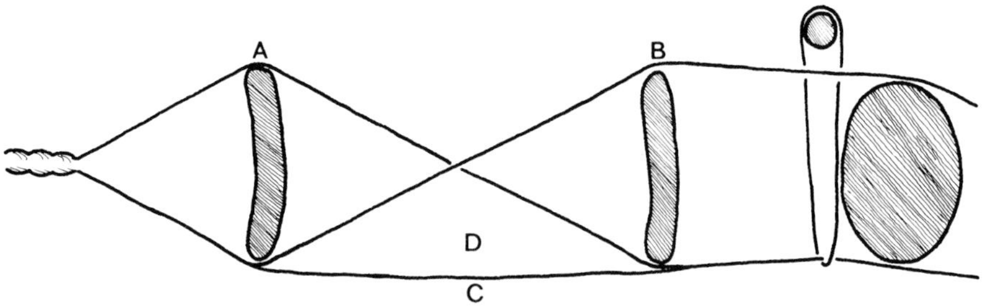

Figure 1. Of the threads from the picked-up shed, the chosen are OVER the first camel rib sword (A) next to the cloth and UNDER the second camel rib sword (B) nearer to the heddles. The discards pass UNDER (A) because they were discarded before it was inserted, and UNDER (B) because of the shed change. All of the threads of the *new* shed pass UNDER (A) and OVER (B). Only the discarded threads (C) bypass the cross formed between the two ribs by the shed change, and float UNDER both of them. Turning the sticks on edge creates a space (D) for passage of the weft in the "X" shed just over the discards.

We can only admire and wonder at the accident, play, error which led to weaving the bottom layer. The solution has such simplicity, directness, elegance. The pleasure of being able to accomplish it so easily is heightened by a keen appreciation of the extremely basic tools.

It might be tempting to speculate about the evolution in the Middle East of this one-weft double cloth from the warp patterned weave in the saha. The textile historian will doubtless shed authoritative light on this. For myself, I like to appreciate the rough gropings of discovery which my imagination insists on portraying:

In the course of weaving, of the weaver's absorption in the rhythms and concentration on the design's development some idea or instinct was triggered. Play or error may have prompted it. The security, comfort, of the routine was nudged and something in the weaver brought her attention and awareness to focus on the implications of it. Discovery is always waiting. Blinded by our need for routine, we are slow to acknowledge and appreciate it. Too often it is cast off as error, irrelevant and unwanted, as we struggle to put ourselves in a dominant role in the weaving process.

We may choose to weave these two techniques in any of several ways. For the purist, romantic, historian, there is the ground loom. Armed with a copy of Crowfoot's articles, tightly spun yarns and sticks from the wood pile, I found this approach was thoroughly satisfying. My appreciation for Bedouin dexterity is matched only by a hope that rigid-heddle-rod ground loom weaving might be more comfortable to those accustomed to working and sitting on the ground.

Photo 4. Working at the ground loom. *Photo, Terry Gritton.*

It is always insightful and informative to execute a weave on the type of loom on which it has been traditionally woven. Subtle nuances of technical refinement and design begin to suggest themselves. It becomes easier to understand the thinking, the intuitions which form the bedrock for its development and for its offshoots. Ideas will come to us which weaving it on our looms would never suggest.

Coming to looms to which we are more accustomed, the most direct translation of this weave is on an inkle or a sturdy two-harness floor loom. (Figures 2 and 3 give the threading.) The inkle also has the unusual permanently fixed

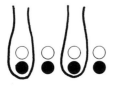

Figure 2. Threading for inkle loom.

Figure 3. Threading for a two harness loom.

Figure 4. Heddling the pair together when threading on a four harness loom.

Figure 5. Separating the pair in the heddles but keeping them on the same harness.

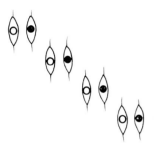

Figure 6. Separating the pair by heddling each thread on a different harness.

heddle position, with counter shed alternately moved above and below the heddle warps to give the two sheds.

Unless the piece is quite narrow (probably less than four inches), shed changing will be difficult — at least if the sett is close enough to satisfy any self-respecting Bedouin. "Snapping" the lower threads through the top ones, about an inch's worth at a time, will help. This is neither difficult nor terribly time consuming for a narrow strip.

For wider cloth, shed changing is unquestionably more expeditious if four or more harnesses are utilized. Several alternatives present themselves for threading this. There are slightly different implications for each threading, as a brief assessment of each will show.

Directly spreading the threading over four harnesses (Fig. 4):
- Is useful for designs where color change is infrequent and gradual, as in wide diagonal stripes, because it maintains the relative positions of light and dark threads within the pair.
- Is quicker to thread than the schemes in Figures 5 and 6 and uses half as many heddles (four pairs require four heddles).
- Offers the most direct relationship between the simplicity of the weave operation and the setup. It is the most "Bedouin-like" of the four-harness versions.

Islolating the colors from each other, but retaining them on the same harness (Fig. 5).
- Is good for the same designing possibilities as mentioned in the assessment of Figure 4.
- May help prevent intertwisting of the threads in the pair unit, particularly when multiple threads of the same color are used as a working unit (for example, *two* lights and *two* darks in the pair).
- Uses twice as many heddles. In a very dense sett, the additional space consumed by the extra number of heddles may be deleterious.

Isolating the colors by harness (Fig. 6).
- Is good for designs where one color predominates or where there are frequent picks of one solid color.
- Takes twice as many heddles and double the threading time for the number of working pairs.
- Is useful when there are multiple threads of each color in the working pair as also in Figure 5.

One can change sheds most easily on a countermarch or counterbalance loom, where the rising harnesses are pulled up and the sinking harnesses simultaneously pulled down. For the countermarch I prefer the tie-up in Figure 7,

Figure 7. Countermarch tie-up for saha and one weft double cloth.

	Treadle 4	Treadle 3	Treadle 2	Treadle 1
Harness 1	O			X
Harness 2		O	X	
Harness 3		X	O	
Harness 4	X			O

O = rising harness

X = sinking harness

For one shed   first treadle 1, so that harness 1 rises, harness 4 falls;
                then treadle 3, so that harness 1 rises, harness 2 falls.
For the counter first treadle 2, so that harness 2 rises, harness 3 falls;
shed   then treadle 4, so that harness 4 rises, harness 4 falls.

which works for all the threading alternatives in Figures 4-6. This is simple and allows the feet to move in a similar fashion to the way the threads and harnesses are moving — creating a certain harmony between technical and physical within the weaving process. Those who have succumbed to the lure of the "universal tie-up" for countermarch treadling need not alter their ways, though the simplicity of the weave may be more difficult to feel. (I find two such tie-ups: Rachel Brown, *The Weaving, Spinning and Dyeing Book*, p. 153; and *The Weaver's Journal*, Vol. 6, No. 3, p. 47. Each requires treadling first harness 4, then 5 for one shed; 6 and then 3 for the counter shed. *The Weaver's Journal* tie-up requires additionally that the threading order of the warps be amended to 1, 3, 2, 4 from the usual 1, 2, 3, 4.)

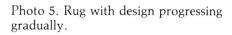

Photo 5. Rug with design progressing
gradually.

On the counterbalance loom one must first modify the loom somewhat by immobilizing the top roller bar or set of pulleys so that harnesses 1 and 2 work independently of 3 and 4. For the one shed, treadle 1, then 3; for the counter shed, 4 and then 2.

In *all* cases the first harness should be raised, and the shed cleared with beater and/or sword before raising the second harness which helps form that shed; whereupon the shed is cleared again. The same principle applies for the counter shed.

If each of these alternatives is treadled in the order as described above, a certain relationship remains constant among harnesses. Both harnesses in each of the plain weave sheds *always* remain in the same orientation to each other when in both top *and* bottom sheds. Harness 1 is always at least slightly above harness 3, 2 slightly above 4. The threads of each harness must pass through the thread layer of the opposite shed, but do not have to endure the additional friction of passing through the threads of the other harness which helps form its own shed.

Because these are complementary warp weaves, whether woven as a double cloth or not they are sleyed almost twice as closely as for ordinary warp face weaving. The warp threads are not able to lie in one horizontal plane in either shed; there is not space enough. Consequently once several picks have been woven, the weaver discovers that those warps picked up for the design the last time *this same* shed was up (e.g., two picks ago) are still slightly atop the discarded threads of that prior pick. This can be seen in Photo 6 and Figure 8. Each pair lies in a vertical plane with the chosen thread on top, the rejected thread underneath, and the faintest suggestion of a space between them. With practice and careful use of pick-up stick this same pick-up row can be retrieved again close to the fell of the cloth.

The pick-up stick bisects this tiny horizontal space or tunnel between the last chosen threads and their discards. Where the design dictates color change, a slight rolling of the appropriate pair between thumb and forefinger will quickly produce the desired color. Once shown where to go by the weaver, the threads become very submissive. They obey their last instructions; they do not anticipate subsequent changes in design. This alignment of the unwoven warps near the fell of the cloth, echoing what has happened so recently to the design in the weaving, seems to be whispering to the weaver to move the design only gradually: "Keep the threads where they want to go; they are falling into place for you. The pattern you are about to create comes from what you have just created."

Thus it is fair to say that pick-up can be greatly expedited if the following conditions are met: density of warp, so that both threads of the pair do not have the space to lie in the same horizontal plane; both colors of the pair being heddled on the same harness so that shed changing does not alter the relative positions of light and dark within the warp pair near the fell of the cloth; selecting the threads close to the fell of the cloth; and a design in which color change occurs in only a few pairs in any one pick.

Care should be taken during pick-up that the two colors in the pair do not become twisted. Twisting has two implications. In the unwoven warp length the twist can be bothersome, particularly if both threads of the pair do not travel through the same heddle. (If they are heddled together, a moderate amount of this twist presents no real problem.) Twisting of the pair has different implications in the cloth. If the dark color was picked up the last time this pair was woven, it ought naturally to be lying slightly on top of its light mate. If the dark is desired again in the current pick-up, it must not be twisted around its light partner. A 360° twist will always appear in the cloth as a noticeable irregularity. However, when a color change occurs (i.e., last time the dark of this pair was chosen; this time the light is needed) the light can be picked up to either left or right of the dark one. If twist has indeed been building up in the unwoven warp length of this pair—either from prior pick-up or from over-twisted warps plying on each other during warping—it can be diminished by a 180° twisting of the light on the appropriate side of the dark.

Photo 6. Picking up the pattern. Note how the placement of color in the unwoven warps near the fell of the cloth echoes the next to last pick (arrow).

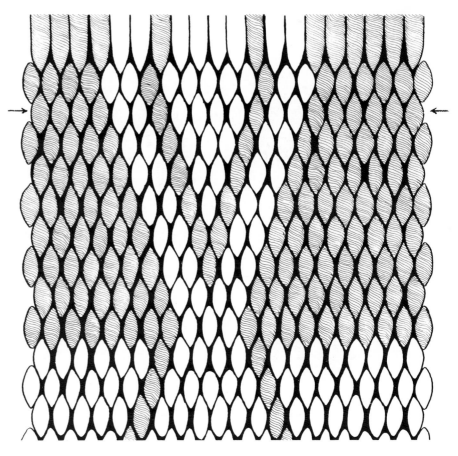

Figure 8. Drawing of the weave showing the character of the color boundaries. Note that the color in the unwoven warps (at top) echo the next to last pick (arrow).

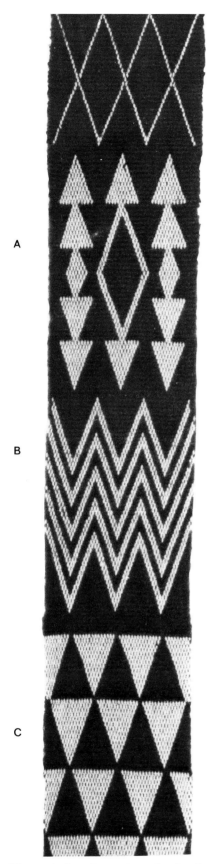

A

B

C

Photo 7. Anne's version of saha designs in commercial black mohair and fawn-colored camel hair. a) Coffee pestle; b) Pigeon's wings; c) Little spears. *Photo, Terry Gritton.*

An error will always show up if a color twists around a thread other than its complementary mate.

Because of the dense warp alignment, one perceives certain qualities about the various color change boundaries: very straight diagonal lines, finely serrated horizontals and undulating verticals (Fig. 8). For those times when designing on paper seems essential, regular square grid paper is not very helpful. It does not begin to capture these qualities with its straight horizontal and vertical lines and stepped diagonals. Cason and Cahlander have thoughtfully introduced the notion of diamond grid paper (p. 184) as a designing aid for weaves with these line characteristics. One can achieve a reasonable approximation of shapes, as they will appear when woven, on this paper. However, diagonal lines will probably be angled differently in the cloth. Design is always strengthened as weaver's intimacy with cloth grows and paper becomes less significant.

For ease of changing sheds, a great deal of tension is needed. A very sturdy loom of four or more harnesses is essential, with good depth between breast and back beams, and between breast beam and harnesses. Countermarch tie-up is preferable. Adding 20-30 pounds of steel bar to the underside of the loom's beater will help facilitate packing in of the wefts without resort to the gazelle horn or its counterpart. When one is using the beater, the reed is its contact surface with the cloth. But reed sizes are very arbitrary and can make weaving impossible if not chosen carefully. A coarsely dented reed is necessary, with several warp pairs sleyed through each dent. The reed will not alter the vertical orientation of warp threads within its dents. Thus the shed change does not move directly down to the fell of the cloth. Placing a sword in the shed in front of the reed before beating will both pack in the previous pick's weft and bring the shed change down to the cloth.

It is difficult to establish the sett well except by trial and error weaving. Thus there may be some discrepancy between the width of the warp as sleyed in the reed and the width it actually wants to be woven in the cloth. Any small discrepancy between these two widths will not be so damaging to the warp threads when bringing the beater forward if the sword intervenes between reed and fell of cloth.

Pick-up sticks or swords should be sturdy, smooth, several inches longer than the width of the cloth and not wider than two inches if possible. When these sticks are turned on edge to expand the "×" shed, the warps are deflected considerably, according to the stick's width.

AFTER SUCH A DELUGE of technical do's and don't's, one might well wonder why anyone who had the choice would select these warp face pick-up weaves. A few words of encouragement may be necessary. Among warp face weaves, severe design limitations within the piece are usual unless pick-up weaves are chosen. The one-weft double cloth's plain weave surfaces are very secure, supple, and luxuriously thick—a rug weaver's delight. Additionally, the saha and one-weft double cloth offer much design freedom—in return for longer weaving time, somewhat comparable to tapestry among weft-faced weaves. Because the cloth develops more slowly than in loom-controlled weaves, the weaver has the time to appreciate the implications and effects of the design as it reveals itself in the cloth. Spontaneity of designing at the loom becomes more comfortable—and more interesting both to weave and to live with.

Initially all is fumbling and confusion. The eyes struggle with learning what to look for, the hands with handling the threads properly. Then the movements are mastered; design begins to reveal itself, hesitantly. Gradually motions begin to flow and rhythms emerge, giving cadence to the work. The threads warm up, become limber, responsive, eager to do as the weaver bids. Pick-up stick and sword learn to penetrate the sheds incisively and accurately. Shed changing becomes rhythmic, second nature. The loom and threads and the weaver's hands work in unison to advance the design into the ever-receding sea of warps. In these motions cloth is born. The weaver's eyes and imagination have time to savor the developing shapes, to alter and enhance them. The rhythms become seductive, compelling the weaver on. Suspense heightens over the resolution of the shapes in the cloth. The elements of time, simple tools, eager threads, weaver's skill enhance each other. Process, meaning and time are wedded.

Photos 8. Anne's version of saha: coffee pestle.

Photo 9. Anne's version of pigeon's wings.

Photo 10. The enchanted, from the author's version of saha.

BIBLIOGRAPHY

Primary descriptions of the saha warp pattern weave and Sudanese camel girth's one-weft double cloth are by:

Crowfoot, Grace M. "The Tent Beautiful: A Study of Pattern Weaving in Transjordan", in *Palestine Exploration Quarterly*. London: January-April, 1945. Pp. 34-47.

-----. "The Sudanese Camel Girth in Double Weave", in *Sudan Notes and Records*. Khartoum: Vol. XXXII, Part 1. June, 1951. Pp. 71-76.

-----. "The Sudanese Camel Girth", in *Kush; Journal of the Sudan Antiquities Service*. Khartoum: Vol. 4, 1956. Pp. 34-38.

A more readily available description of the two weaves can be found in:

Collingwood, Peter. *The Techniques of Rug Weaving*. New York: Watson-Guptill, 1968. Pp. 449-451, pl. 147.

Precise structural descriptions of the two weaves have been done by:

Emery, Irene. *The Primary Structures of Fabrics; An Illustrated Classification*. Washington, D.C.: The Textile Museum, 1966. P. 145 for saha, 155, 158 for one-weft double cloth.

Rowe, Ann Pollard. *Warp-Patterned Weaves of the Andes*. Washington, D.C.: The Textile Museum, 1977. P. 50 for saha, 94 for one-weft double cloth.

Much information on rigid heddle rod ground looms and weaving women can be found in the next two references. The first also has numerous photos of saha curtains. Neither gives information on weaving saha.

Weir, Shelagh. *The Bedouin: Aspects of the Material Culture of the Bedouin of Jordan*. London: World of Islam Festival, 1976.

-----. *Spinning and Weaving in Palestine*. London: British Museum, 1970.

For a description of weaving one-weft double cloth as done in Bolivia, as well as diamond grid paper, see:

Cason, Marjorie and Adele Cahlander. *The Art of Bolivian Highland Weaving*. New York: Watson-Guptill, 1976. Pp. 77-81, 120-122, 184.

Photo 1. Brocade pendant edged with braid. *Shoso-in Repository, Nara, Japan. 8th century.*

Photo 2. Suit of armor. Heian period.

When I first met Anne Blinks she was working out old Peruvian braiding structures on an ingenious round stand perfectly suited to the task and to her comfort, a stand designed before she had become familiar with the Japanese tradition of braiding and its use of such stands (see p. 120 for photo of her stand). I had been forewarned of the scope of her knowledge and the keenness of her mind. I remember that, as we sat and talked, I was particularly impressed by the pleasure she took in the intricacies of a textile fragment, her fascination with human ingenuity, her deep respect for the makers of things, her interest in my own work and her provocative questions. For all this I have been very grateful.

BRAIDING IN JAPAN

BY MARY DUSENBURY

Introduction

The braider sits on his knees in formal Japanese fashion in front of the round hardwood stand. His back is straight as he bends forward from the hips and his hands move quickly over the stand lifting successive pairs of silk elements—lead-weighted bobbins dangling—and repositioning them surely and swiftly. He watches his work with intense concentration as the smooth silk elements dance into position. Counterweighted, the finished braid moves slowly down through the beveled central opening and the scales of its pattern shimmer as it lies slithering on the floor by his knees. The silence is broken only by an occasional thud, thud of bobbin hitting bobbin or the squeak of silk as he repositions elements on the stand after the conclusion of a repeat. Our braider might be demonstrating at an exhibition of traditional textile crafts or he might be putting in a day's work at one of the famous old braiding houses in the districts around Tokyo, Nagoya, Kyoto or Kanazawa. If our braider were a woman, she would more probably have a pot of rice steaming in the background and a child or grandchild playing with an extra bobbin on the tatami-matted floor of her dwelling. She might be an out-braider for a braiding house, or she might work independently, selling directly to specialty shops and supplying herself and her family with ties for clothing and for a woman's *obi*-sash. *Obijime* (or *obishime*) and *obidome*, the little braids that, today, encircle the wide hard *obi*-sash worn with a woman's kimono are the major product of contemporary braiding houses and of independent braiders alike.

The braider and his stand have been a familiar part of the Japanese textile world for a millenium. Most of the hundreds of fine 8th century braids preserved in the Todaiji Temple's Shoso-in Repository in Nara appear to have been done on stands very similar to the round and square stands in use today. These stands, with their system of weighted bobbins and counterweights, were probably introduced to Japan from T'ang China (T'ang: A.D. 618-907) in the late 7th or the 8th century with the influx of Chinese Buddhism, culture, political structure and art that characterized the late Asuka and the Nara periods in Japan (Asuka: 552-710; Nara: 710-794). As braiding is a subsidiary textile skill, its documentation through the ages has been scanty at best, but bits of braids, often attached to clothing or other objects preserved in temples, shrines or graves, as well as old paintings and a very occasional literary reference make it amply clear that this tradition has been unbroken from the time of its introduction to the Japanese islands to the present day and also that there have been interesting variations from period to period as braiders have responded to the needs of the times and to changing aesthetic sensibilities.

Braids have always been made for a specific purpose and with a keen awareness of the interrelationship of structure and function. They are sturdier than twisted cords and were undoubtedly first developed for their strength. Clay imprints of braids have been found from the early Jomon period (Jomon: 7000-250 B.C.), long before the introduction of a complex tradition of silk braiding from the continent.

In the Shoso-in collection, most braids are found attached to other objects. They serve as ties for clothing, as they still do today. They lace the ends and center section of drums together and allow the drummer to hold his drum with ease. They are attached to the edges of scrolls of Buddhist scripture and keep them rolled neatly when not in use. They dangle as ornament from a very beautiful harp and are often used to finish the edges of a woven piece. Fragments of brocade-covered pads and pendants are edged with scallops of flat braids which both strengthen the borders and add to the visual complexity so characteristic of the Nara period (Photo 1). Beginning in the late Heian period (Heian: 794-1185) and particularly from the military-dominated Kamakura period onwards (Kamakura: 1185-1336), braids became closely associated with military culture. Most of the many styles of armor were composed of rows of metal or lacquer plaques bound together with strong, flat, flexible braids and edged with hard, tight ones (Photo 2). Swords and hilts were wrapped and bound in braids — leggings tied with braids — and horses and oxen decked in braided, knotted and fringed coverings — at least for festive occasions (Photo 3). Later the warrior-sponsored tea ceremony also used braids — to hang and to tie scrolls and as ties for elegant brocaded coverings of tea ceremony utensils.

Photo 3. Head of ox in festival trappings. Aoi Matsuri. Contemporary. *Photographer, Frances Skinner.*

Photo 4. Detail of priest's costume. Fushimi Inari Shrine fire festival. Contemporary. *Photographer, Frances Skinner.*

As part of an effort to alter the social as well as political system, the Meiji government (Meiji: 1868-1912) forbade the wearing of swords (a distinction used for centuries to set the samurai apart from the commoner). This prohibition with all it entailed seemed, for a time, to be a death knell to the fine old braiding houses as well as to other more obviously military-related craftsmen. Even the continuing demands of temples, shrines, traditional theater (Noh, Kabuki and Bunraku), and the tea ceremony seemed insufficient to assure the future of the braiding houses. It was at this point that the most innovative of the old craftsmen turned their skills to making *obijime* and promoted their usefulness and visual appeal so successfully that, today, the industry is again flourishing.

When I returned to Japan in 1974 to study at the College of Arts in Kyoto, I searched for a place to study these braids. Finally I found a little school, the Miyabi School of Braiding, which turned out to be a large tatami-matted room at the top of a very steep stairway with big windows overlooking bustling Shijo street in downtown Kyoto. (Later I also received a great deal of help from a very fine braiding house in Otsu, on the outskirts of Kyoto.) The school's four courses took about 14 months to complete. Every week, for half a day, we assembled and were taught a new braid. We worked both on the round stand and on the closely related square stand. When I started, most of the braids were unpublished, their intricacies carefully guarded both by the braiding houses and by small schools such as Miyabi. Sometime in the mid-70's, one school published a few diagrams and immediately the market was deluged with braiding books as the same institutions hurried to be first in the bookshops. Some of these books are quite good and by now the most important of the old braids have been published. A great many, of course, still have not.

Despite the rash of recent publications and an upsurge of popular interest in braiding, there has been no studied attempt to present the braids in a framework that elucidates their basic structures and methods of construction. Their names, whether straightforward or whimsical, suggest a miscellany of shape, pattern, place and historical figures. At the end of my first study, my notebooks seemed a jumbled array of miscellaneous constructions. A search for a framework within which to interpret my imposing mass of slithering little braids led to Irene Emery, Raoul d'Harcourt and Issei Yamaoka. I found that although a number of the braids could be fitted into one system or another, none of these systems seemed to respect the integrity of the tradition nor to provide a useful framework within which to understand the ways that these particular braids are put together nor the interrelationships, the kinship patterns as it were, of my basketful of problems.

There is a very close relationship between structure and method of construction in the Japanese tradition and thus between structure and tool. Over the centuries, the old stands with their weights and counterweights have significantly affected the development of new braids by determining the ways that elements can move and ways that they cannot. It seemed to me that a system of classification based on the movement of elements as they interlace to form the finished braid, a system drawn from the tradition itself and from a braider's perspective, would provide a useful and flexible framework within which to understand and interpret this tradition known, in Japan, as kumihimo (kumi- or gumi-group; himo-string, cord).

In this paper, I will attempt to describe some of the major characteristics of the tradition including the important relationship of tool to structure. I will conclude with a preliminary classification of the major categories of braids based on the criteria outlined above and with a small but representative sample of braids for each category. I hope that the framework this provides will give the reader an overview of the ways that braids are put together and the information necessary to begin to understand the thinking of the Japanese braider.

About the Braids

Several years ago, a year or two after I had started working with the sleek, smooth Japanese braids, Junius Bird gave me the opportunity to spend several fascinating days with his collection of Peruvian braids in the Museum of Natural History in New York. I remember responding almost hungrily to the rich use of texture in these braids—the skillful use of twist, of thickness of element—great heavy cords working in with lighter, more delicate ones to provide a textural feast for viewer, user and handler. Although many of the actual braiding structures seemed very similar to those of certain old braids in Japan, the feeling of the two traditions is radically different, a difference derived less from structure than from materials, function and the intent of the braider and aesthetic sensibilities of his culture.

MATERIALS. The preferred material, and the material for which most Japanese braiding structures are devised, is silk. The silk is reeled from several cocoons together to form fine long strong filaments which, after degumming, have a lustrous shine. These filaments have little or no twist and are used many together to form one braiding element. A four-element braid for an *obijime* (of approximately ¾cm diameter) has about 70 filaments per element, whereas a braid of roughly equal diameter but with more elements (any multiple of four up to about 36 on a square or round stand) has many fewer filaments per element and is worked with comparably lighter bobbin weights.

Other materials are sometimes used such as ramie, occasionally cotton and, recently, a man-made fiber called *biron* which was developed specifically to imitate the braiding qualities of silk. None of these, however, is as good as silk. Silk is lustrous, smooth, a little slippery and very strong. A finished silk braid has tremendous strength and yet is lightweight. It can be either very flexible or quite hard and firm. It will hold a knot well—an important consideration when lashing a sword or tying an *obijime*.

TEXTURE. Despite the obvious design potential of the use of different types of materials or of contrasting thick and thin elements within a single braid, the design possibilities of texture have almost never been explored. Very occasionally one finds a braid in which the elements are not of equal weight, in which some are composed of more silk filaments than others, but in these braids bobbin weights are changed to effectively eliminate any textural difference the use of larger and smaller elements might naturally produce. In fact braiders take great pains to eliminate any textural variation either within the elements or between elements.

A great deal of attention, however, is given to the degree and direction of twist.

TWIST. Although each silk filament has little or no twist, in many braids the whole element is given a twist as it is being worked. This twist may be strong, medium or weak and may be in either direction. Generally, if a twist is given, some of the elements are twisted 'S' and others 'Z' within the same braid. Some braids use no twist at all. The degree and direction of twist, or conversely, the absence of twist, are considered to be an important part of the construction of any given braid.

A few of the lovely old *karagumi (kara*-old Chinese) flat plaits in the Shoso-in collection are worked with elements comprised of two heavy silk cords each, one twisted 'Z' and one 'S'. Apparently it takes great skill for a braider to work such elements smoothly. The effect is of fine braided cords worked into a larger braided structure (Photo 5).

DESIGN AND PATTERN. The structure of the braid, the materials it is made from, the texture of the elements and the degree and direction of their twist all contribute to the design of the finished braid. None of these, however, can vie with the manipulation of color for immediate visual impact. Great care and skill have always been given to the combination, gradation and juxtaposition of color within individual braids and attention paid to the effect produced by a mass of braids seen together as in armor or a contemporary window display. Each color is carefully selected and so skillfully dyed that today, over a thousand years later, some of the early Shoso-in braids still seem very beautiful.

There has always been a keen awareness of the ways in which a braiding structure affects the color or colors used, of the visual interrelationship of structure and color. Color, and its use with certain braiding structures, has been used to indicate rank. It can draw attention to a particularly interesting braiding structure that, otherwise, as a small accoutrement to another object or group of objects, might pass unnoticed. Even some very simple structures, such as *marugenji* (braids 7 and 8), allow a variety of patterns depending on the number of elements, the colors used and their placement at the start of the braid. Some braiding structures seem to enhance a gentle gradation of shades while others effectively set off sharp juxtapositions of hue.

Silk, which dyes perhaps best of all natural fibers, has allowed the full exploitation of color, while the use of a multitude of tiny filaments to comprise each braiding element adds depth and interest to the total effect.

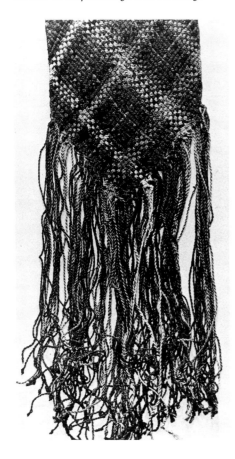

Photo 5. Plait with paired elements, one 'Z' and one 'S'. 7.2cm×214.4cm. *Shoso-in Repository. 8th century.*

Working Methods

Here we must return to our braider, formally seated at his stand, with quietly poised body and quickly moving arms and hands. Both left and right hands have equal work and must move at equal speed and with equal tension. The braider reaches low to lift the ends of the elements to keep the bobbins from flying and tangling as his hands dance out the structure of the braid. The work of tensioning is left to the weighted bobbins as, released by the hands, they fall naturally into place. Only occasionally do the hands purposefully tension the elements or tighten a braid.

The elements are always handled in pairs and generally move in a pattern that is then repeated, often in the opposite direction, by another pair. Diagonal opposites are often worked together, neighbors and/or opposites. No element is ever worked alone.

To set up the braid, the braider carefully smooths the fine silk filaments comprising each element, filaments which have been reeled, degummed, dyed and measured into units of the appropriate length and number. When each filament lies flat against its neighbor, the braider winds the element on a weighted bobbin finishing with a half-hitch that will enable the bobbin to slide down the element as more braiding room is required. The other ends of the elements are knotted together and either counterweighted through the opening in the center of the round stand or placed on a square or rectangular metal tongue and counterweighted to be worked up from the center of the square stand. The bobbins are then carefully adjusted so that they fall an equal distance down the sides of the stand and the appropriate twist is put in. To do this, the braider gives the bobbin a sharp twist in the direction required and allows it to spin freely until it is adequately twisted. He then stops it with his hand. As the twist extends only from the center of the stand to the bobbin, it must be reapplied every few minutes as the braid is worked.

Fast as he works, the braider carefully monitors the evenness of the braid as it grows and the smoothness of each element. Should even a single filament get out of place in the course of the braiding, the braider will stop, undo the bobbin, smooth the filaments and rewind them before continuing. Set-up and the time taken to keep the elements smooth can easily surpass the actual braiding time of a skillful braider.

The use of weighted bobbins and a stand to support the elements leaves both hands free to work quickly while making a firm, well-balanced construction. It also allows for the easy manipulation of elements composed of a multitude of tiny filaments. As in any braid, since elements move independently, structures and/or patterns may be changed in the course of the braid.

Tools

Tools are very important. We invent or adopt tools to enable us to do a specific job more quickly or to do a complex job a little more easily. The tools that we build in turn affect our thinking and, especially, the thinking of our successors for whom they become an integral part of an inherited tradition. The tool may suggest new developments of structure or methods of working which in turn can lead to new adaptations of the tool. As it becomes more complex, it must often become more specific and less flexible. While such a tool opens some options, it closes others.

The two oldest as well as most versatile stands in use today are the round stand and the square stand. Both were almost certainly in common use by the 8th century. Later other stands were developed to cater to a particular type of braid enabling it to be worked more efficiently and, often, permitting a complexity that would be difficult — or very time-consuming — on a simpler stand (multi-element two-layered plaiting on the *taka-dai*; warp-twined structures on the *ayatake-dai* (see Figures 1 and 2)). This increase in efficiency and complexity, however, is offset by a corresponding loss of flexibility, an inverse relationship somewhat comparable to that found when one compares a back-strap loom, a floor loom and a Jacquard.

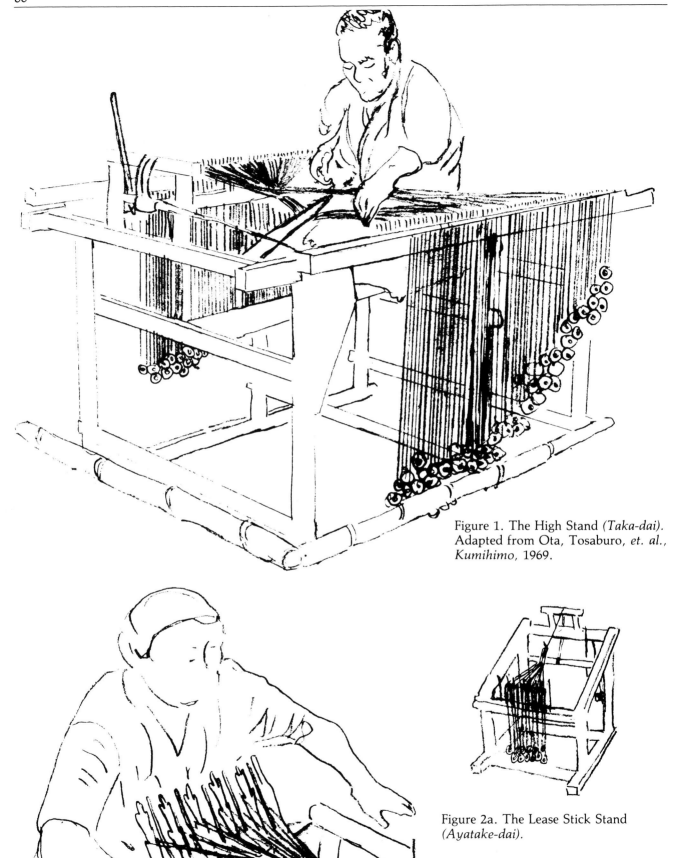

Figure 1. The High Stand *(Taka-dai)*. Adapted from Ota, Tosaburo, *et. al.*, *Kumihimo*, 1969.

Figure 2a. The Lease Stick Stand *(Ayatake-dai)*.

Figure 2b. Detail of *Ayatake-dai*. Adapted from Ota, Tosaburo, *et. al.*, *Kumihimo*, 1969.

THE ROUND STAND *(Maru-dai)* (Photo 6). The round stand is composed of a circular wooden disk on four legs and a base. It is about 16" high. The disk on a contemporary round stand has a beveled opening in the center and is made of very fine quality close-grained hardwood with a smooth finish. The working elements must be able to slide quickly and freely over the surface with no danger of catching on the wood. The braid can be worked either 'up' or 'down'. Today, it is generally counterweighted through the opening at the center of the stand and moves down as the braid grows 'up'. The unworked elements, on their weighted bobbins, fan out from the center of the braid to the edges of the stand and dangle around the edges. These elements can move freely either *around* or *through* the central core of the braid as it grows, making this stand the most versatile of all stands. In fact most, if not all, of the braids in the very large portfolio of a professional braider could probably be done on this simple stand.

A typical round stand today has a disk of about a 10" diameter which will accommodate a 28-element braid. The small diameter is desirable, as it strains the braider's back much less than a larger stand. Somewhat larger disks are also fairly common, enabling a braider to work up to 36 strands with relative ease. I have seen photographs of enormous disks of four or five feet in diameter. These obviously require many braiders. Rare today, they were probably used in the past whenever particularly large braids were needed — as for horse and oxen trappings, decorative adjuncts to portable shrines, etc.

A contemporary mechanized version of such a monster is the wooden *naiki-dai* (stand with inner working mechanisms) which has an ingenious

Photo 6. The Round Stand *(Maru-dai)*.

Photo 7. The Square Stand *(Kaku-dai)*.

mechanical system of levers that automatically move an element over one or several of its neighbors and then the adjacent one back in a comparable movement (see category I braiding structures). The inherent lack of interest in the simple, though quite serviceable, structures this 'machine' clatters out is sometimes alleviated by adding a small handworked section which uses different elements, different colors, and, sometimes, a different structure. This section might well be a particularly visible portion of an *obijime*. A core of potential working elements is hung over the central opening and used as a core around which the *naiki* elements move. For most of the braid it is completely encased and merely serves to make the braid a little firmer than it would otherwise be. To add the patterned area, the braider moves the core elements to working position and works them by hand into the pattern desired, often using the main working elements as a core for the length of the hand-braided area. Of course such a core can be used with the simple round stand as well.

When the hands lift, move, and set down a pair of elements, they have moved them through the *inside*, the core, of the braid.

THE SQUARE STAND *(Kaku-dai)* (Photo 7). The square stand is a square platform of similar fine-grained hardwood on four legs and a base. It also is 16" high. A contemporary square stand often has two interchangeable tables, one with approximately 4" sides, the other with 8" sides. The small table can accommodate only a 4- or 8-element braid, but is very quick and easy to work with. The larger table can handle as many as 32 or 36 working elements. Unlike the contemporary round stand, the square stand does not have a central opening. The braid is counterweighted to move up as it is worked 'down' and the portion being worked rests on a small metal tongue set into the center of the stand. The tongue is either square or rectangular, depending on the shape of the braid desired.

Working elements on weighted bobbins fan out from the center of the braid to the four sides of the stand and hang around the edges as on the round stand. It is obviously much easier to keep track of a multi-element braid if the elements are clearly divided into quadrants than if they are arranged evenly around a circular disk. This is particularly true if the braider is working a monochromatic braid with a multitude of evenly spaced elements. Some structures are quicker to work on this stand than on the round one and some are firmer, partly perhaps because of the central metal tongue. However, working elements obviously cannot move through the core of the braid so that structures on this stand are limited to ones in which the elements move *around* the central core.

When the hands lift, move and reposition a pair of elements, they have moved them *around* the central core.

The late master braider, Jusuke Fukami, who was given the coveted title of Holder of Intangible Cultural Properties for his fine wide *karagumi* sashes *(hirao)*, sometimes used an interesting variation of the square stand. A wooden frame set on legs, with the far side slightly higher than the side near the braider, it had an open center and pegs around the sides of the frame to hold the braiding elements in place.

The round stand and the square stand with braid working up or down are really two variations on a common theme. The two other stands in common use today, however, are each quite different in conception.

THE HIGH STAND *(Taka-dai)* (Fig. 1). The high stand is a tall three-sided frame used to produce flat plaited structures (diagonal interlacement). Its two opposite sides are surmounted by a row of closely spaced pegs between which the working elements hang to dangle on the outside of the stand. The braider kneels on a platform between the two rows of pegs facing the front bar over which the finished braid passes to be wound around a small beam quite similar in concept to the cloth beam of a loom. The high stand can accommodate many more working elements than a round stand operated by one person and its pegs keep any number of elements properly positioned. Most wide plaits can be worked more quickly, smoothly and evenly on the high stand than on the round stand. If fitted with an additional row of pegs on either side of the braider, the high stand also facilitates the production of complex double-layered plaits that would be extremely difficult to execute on a round stand.

The most important braid that is generally worked on the high stand is the *hirao*, a horizontal as well as vertical multiple of diagonal interlacements and their reversals. The *hirao* is a wide, flat plait, approximately 10cm by 2m, which may have between 300 and 400 working elements. The braid known today as *karagumi* is a one-unit version of this and is commonly worked with 28 elements. It is one of the oldest and most beloved of the round stand braids and is a favorite for the most elegant of the handworked *obijime*. The *obijime karagumi* may be worn by anyone who can afford it. Use of the *hirao*, however, is restricted to members of the court nobility, Gagaku dancers (dancers to the Imperial Court), high Shinto priests and a few other privileged people. Although similar braids used for pendant ornaments and sashes were introduced to Japan from China in the 7th century, even before the Nara period, the braid known today as the *hirao* is most closely associated with the costume and customs of the Heian period, the period of high court culture. Originally a sword belt, it is now worn almost exclusively as a ceremonial sash hanging from the front of the waist to mid-calf. Center and borders are generally worked differently. The center may have fine gradations of color achieved through prior space-dyeing of the elements and sometimes overlaid with stitchery while border areas make full use of the pattern possibilities of the structure itself.

It is not known exactly when the high stand was developed or imported, but it seems fairly clear that it was sometime after the Nara period. There are a number of wide, flat *karagumi* plaits (see Photo 5) in the Shoso-in collection that, today, would be done on a high stand. However, the *taka-dai* produces a flat cross section and all of the plaits in the Shoso-in have what Issei Yamaoka in *Shoso-in no Kumihimo* describes as an 'inward-warped cross section' (a flat braid which curves inward at both edges), a trait that is typical of such braids when they are worked on a round stand.

Whether in Japan or on the continent, the high stand was undoubtedly developed to expedite the production of such flat plaits and to permit them to be worked wider. It is completely different in concept from the round stand. Working methods are so unlike that an inexperienced braider working a structure first on the round stand and then on the high stand might well not recognize that he was working a similar structure — although the two products might be almost indistinguishable to the eye. A tool has its own exigencies and makes its own suggestions. On the high stand, the simple addition of another row of pegs on either side of the braider, for instance, creates new possibilities of structural variation and of patterning that would be so unreasonably difficult to execute on a round stand that they would probably never have been imagined.

One can hypothesize that a demand for a wider and flatter sash than those in the Shoso-in led to the invention or, more probably, introduction of a prototype of the high stand and a completely different method of working the plaits. One can further imagine that, in the course of time, the movement of elements on this *taka-dai* suggested new structural variations to the hands of the braider. The development of double-layered plaiting is an obvious example and the addition of a second row of pegs, to accommodate the second layer, a natural modification of the stand. The emergence of the high stand as an important tool with its own repertory of braiding structures has not yet been documented, but the appearance in the Heian period of the *hirao*, a consistently wider plait than most in the Shoso-in and one in which a flat cross section is of considerable importance, suggests that a prototype, at least, of the *taka-dai* was introduced to Japan sometime in the late Nara or the early Heian period. Can one see a further development of this stand in the appearance of a few very complex double-layered tortoise-shell patterned braids in the succeeding Kamakura period?

More important for our purposes here, however, than attempting to date the introduction of a particular stand, is the close interrelationship that such a development suggests between braiding structure and stand, an inter-dependency that seems quite typical of this particular braiding tradition. In fact, such a sensitive and fertile interaction between textile structures and the tools of their production may be seen as an important theme throughout the long course of Japanese textile history.

THE LEASE STICK STAND (*Ayatake-dai*) or STAND FROM SURUGA (*Suruga-dai*). (Fig. 2). On this stand 'warp' elements twine around each other as they move between the grooves and the base of the stand while the double 'weft' serves to hold the twine in place. Many stands have just one set of grooves, but others have two. I don't know whether more than two are ever used. The warp-twined structures produced on this ingenious stand have sometimes been mistaken for tablet weaving, which was not known in Japan until very recently.

There is another, very simple, stand that would seem to produce warp-twined structures. Not in use today, it is known from its depiction in a Muromachi period scroll painting (Muromachi: 1336-1568) and scholars write only that it is "very old" and that it can produce "quite complex braids". The stand does not use a system of weights and counterweights but organizes the elements in looped pairs manipulated and tensioned by the braider (Photo 8).*

There are other braiding stands, but the *maru-dai* and the *kaku-dai* (the round and square stands), the *taka-dai* and the *ayatake-dai* are by far the most important of the stands used today.

Photo 8. Figure of woman braiding from the scroll painting, *Nanajuichiban Shokunin Uta Awase no E.* Muromachi period.

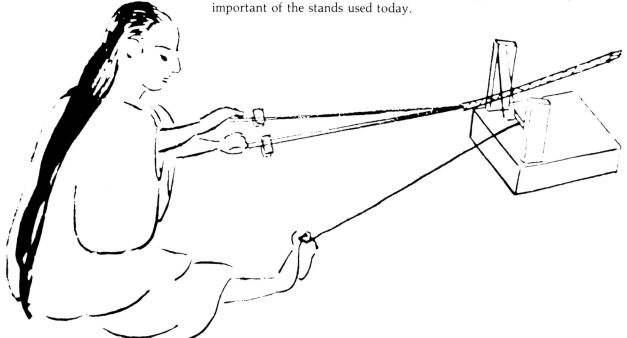

BOBBINS. The bobbins that hold the working elements are made of a smooth, fine-grained hardwood with heavy lead plugs. They are of various weights which correspond to the number of working elements in the braid and the number of filaments in each working element. Different braiding houses use slightly different weights which means that some houses work their braids under a little more tension than others. The heaviest bobbins I have worked with weigh approximately 30 ounces (210 'monmei' in the old system of weights which is still used for braiding tools). These are used for counter-weights on the round stand and for working a four-element *obijime* braid with approximately 70 filaments per working element. A very common weight is about 10 ounces, and the smallest bobbins I have used weigh only 4 ounces.

*This stand is referred to and the figure represented in Domyo, Shinbe-e, *Himo* and Ota, Tosaburo, et. al., *Kumihimo*. It calls to mind Mariann Cardale-Schrimpff's "reciprocal braiding" and Noémi Speiser's "loop manipulation" which are discussed in Speiser, Noémi, "The Techniques and the Methods of Braiding", *CIETA Bulletin*, 1977, #46.

OTHER TOOLS. Many tools for winding, sorting and measuring fine silk threads that are common in a silk weaver's workshop are also found in a braider's: reels, reel winders, skein winders, etc. There are also a small number of specialized tools such as one for holding the end of an *obijime* braid while its end fringes are being worked, as well as dye equipment. I won't attempt to enumerate or describe these here as they have little to do with the basic construction of the braids.

Braiding Structures
The Choreography of a Braid

A braider working on a stand has a certain repertory of movements with which to construct his braid and he learns to think, and his hands to work, within the framework imposed by this repertory.

The braids are always composed of groups of elements. The very smallest group is a pair, the pair that is worked together for that moment. That pair might work together throughout the braid as two parts of one whole, or each element might, in the course of the braiding, form a pair with a new element. The distinction is not important. A slightly larger group is often a pair of pairs—an opposite diagonal pair worked in one direction, for instance, and its 'neighbors', the elements that the hands naturally touch on completion of the first movement, in an opposite. Some groups of braids (most of category I) are composed of two basic sets—one moving clockwise, the other counterclockwise. Others, although they are divided into quadrants on the stand, are best understood as two sets of elements with opposite groups comprising two halves of one set (most of category III). The braids d'Harcourt would call 'plaiting-weaving' also have two sets of elements, a 'warp' set and a 'weft' set (category III B). A very few braids, such as *Hirakakugumi* (braid 6, category II), just have one set. Others have more than two. *Kakugenji* ([Prince] Genji's square [braid]) has four sets. The first two sets move as a category III B braid but with two 'warp' sets, the second two in a manner similar to braid 7, category II *(Marugenji)*. The four sets move alternately, one pair, or pair of pairs, at a time.

The use of weighted bobbins necessitates balanced movements. When I first started looking at a few of the braids in the Peruvian collection of the American Museum of Natural History in New York, I was fascinated by structural similarities to old braids that I was seeing in Japan. Then I was perhaps even more intrigued by the seeming eccentricities of certain elements in the Peruvian braids. I would expect them to move in a certain fashion which they, almost impishly, would refuse to do. Weights and counterweights have their own requirements which become so much second nature to the braider that it becomes difficult to think in different terms.

If heavy weights dangle freely around a stand they *must* be worked in a fashion that keeps the counterweighted center braid centered. Movements from left (L) to right (R) are naturally and quickly followed by countermovements from R to L to maintain the balance. In category IV braids such as *koamigumi* (braid 12), the *Genji* braids (braid 11) and other "woven braids", the 'weft' can never be a single element but must always consist of at least two elements, one L and one R, which form the 'weft' by changing position with each other through the 'open shed' of the 'warp' elements. Although it might be perfectly possible for such a braid to have a single 'weft' in another braiding system, it is impossible in this counterweighted system; and no braider would ever imagine working such a braid. The L and R elements are really two parts of one element. Eliminating one is inconceivable. While this system forbids the use of a single 'weft', however, it encourages the use of additional 'weft' pairs. With smooth silk as material and heavy weights for tension, two, four or even eight 'wefts' can be used and still be easily covered by the 'warp'. Thus one finds nice variations of woven-braids, variations in which the 'weft' elements interplay with each other instead of simply acting as 'weft', thus thickening and strengthening the braid and its edges as well as adding a good deal of interest to the borders.

A Preliminary Classification of Braiding Structures

I have divided the braids into four major categories according to the ways that the elements move to construct the braid and to the interrelationship of different sets of elements. This classification is made from the perspective of a braider who watches the braid as it grows rather than from that of a scholar analyzing a finished cross section. The categories are meant to clarify the ways in which braids are put together. I do not intend them to be definitive.

The following diagrams are for braids made today on the round or the square stand to be used as *obijime*. Some of the braids are very old, while others are recent variations created in response to a search for variety in a fast-paced marketplace. From this large repertory I have chosen a few braids from each category to illustrate the basic constructions of braids that are made today on the round and the square stands and of the types of variations that grow out of them.

In reading the diagrams, it is important to remember that on the round stand elements move through the inside of the braid while on the square stand they move around the outside. As the finished braid descends through the center opening on the round stand it is growing 'up'. The reverse is true for the square stand.

Definition of Terms

In the notes accompanying the diagrams, I will use the following terms:

Element: A group of (silk) filaments wound together on a bobbin.

Set: A group of elements that interact with one another during the course of the braiding. A braid may be composed of one, two, three, four or more sets. Two is the most common. There may be some movement of elements between sets.

Step: The completed movement of a pair of bobbins from one position to another. The step is over when the hands release the bobbins to pick up another pair.

Sequence: A given number of steps which, when repeated, will produce a particular braiding structure. It is possible for a braid to be composed of more than one braiding sequence.

Repeat: The number of sequences necessary to return each element to its starting position.

The Braids

Figure 3: Putting in the twist. Elements are twisted toward the nearest corner with the side of the bobbin away from the stand turning first towards the corner. To do this, the 'bottom' right bobbin must turn counterclockwise, "S", and the 'top' right must turn clockwise, "Z". If there is more than one element in a quadrant, both are given the same twist towards the same corner. The twist may be hard, medium or light. Generally, although not always, all elements are given the same degree of twist but not the same direction. As the twist extends only from the center of the stand to the bobbin, it must be reapplied when the bobbin is lengthened.

Unless otherwise noted, all square stand braids in the following diagrams are given a twist as indicated in this diagram. Round stand braids are not.

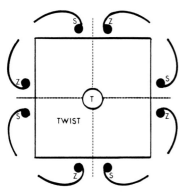

Figure 3. Putting in the twist.

CATEGORY I: Movement *around* a (hollow) core with two sets of elements, one moving clockwise, one counterclockwise.

In the majority of category I braids, each element moves 360° around the core to return to its starting position within the repeat.

Braid 1. This is the basic category I braid. It can be done with more elements but each set must have an equal, and even, number of elements. *Edoyatsu* requires two sequences, (1-4)×2, to make one repeat.

With the addition of a few bows and curtseys, a multi-element version of this braid also forms the core of the English Maypole dances. Actually any of

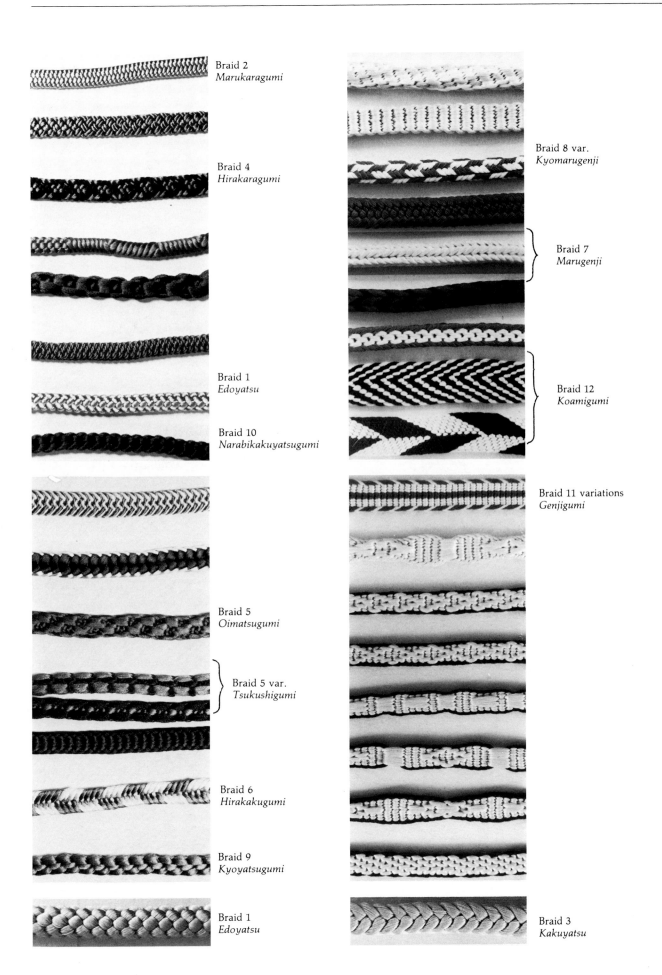

Braid 2
Marukaragumi

Braid 4
Hirakaragumi

Braid 1
Edoyatsu

Braid 10
Narabikakuyatsugumi

Braid 5
Oimatsugumi

Braid 5 var.
Tsukushigumi

Braid 6
Hirakakugumi

Braid 9
Kyoyatsugumi

Braid 1
Edoyatsu

Braid 8 var.
Kyomarugenji

Braid 7
Marugenji

Braid 12
Koamigumi

Braid 11 variations
Genjigumi

Braid 3
Kakuyatsu

94

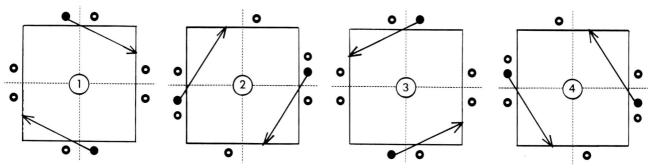

Braid 1: *Edoyatsu.*

the braids in this section, any braid worked around a core (the pole) in which the braid is worked 'down', can be danced around a maypole (or any other convenient pole for that matter).

(*Edoyatsu*—eight-element (braid) from Edo—an old name for Tokyo.)

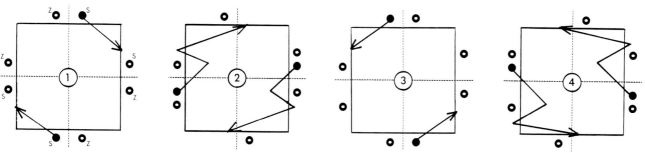

Braid 2: *Marukaragumi.*

Braid 2. This braid has the same basic structure as Braid 1 although it is worked with 16 elements instead of with eight and each working element moves over two passive elements instead of over one.

(*Marukaragumi*—round Chinese-style braid.)

Multi-element versions of Braids 1 and 2 are among the most common structures produced on the *naiki-dai*.

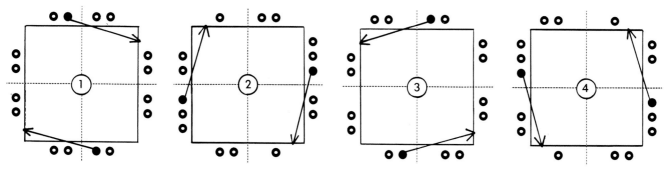

Braid 3: *Kakuyatsu.*

Braid 3. To form a square version of the basic category I braid, the two pairs of elements at the 'top' and 'bottom' of the stand are transposed (Fig. 4) before braiding starts which places elements of like twist at each corner. At (2) and (4), the working elements are taken from *under* their neighbors so that they enter the core of the braid. They then pass over (outside) a second passive element. This movement is indicated by a jagged arrow. Steps (1) and (3) have no structural significance as the moving elements do not interwork with other elements. They are repositioned on the stand to keep the braid balanced and even and to facilitate the working of the braid.

(Kakuyatsu — square, eight-element (braid).)

Figure 4. Set-up for Braid 3.

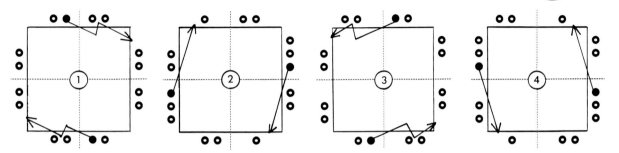

Braid 4: *Hirakaragumi.*

Braid 4. This distinctive braid differs from Braid 2 only in that at steps (1) and (2) working elements move 'under one-over one' [as in Braid 3, steps (2) and (4)] instead of 'over two'. This change alters the shape of the braid from a simple round structure to a rectangularly elongated one tapering gently toward the edges, an effect which is usually enhanced by the use of a rectangular metal tongue instead of a square one. This braid sets off pattern very well and a number of variations can be made by changing the number and placement of the colors. It seems most appropriate for two-color patterns. It is often made with only a very gentle twist.

(Hirakaragumi — flat Chinese-style braid.)

The pattern possibilities of Braid 4 may be increased by adding one pair of elements to each quadrant to make a 24-element braid. In this Kyoto-style version of the braid, *Kyohirakaragumi,* elements pass under one and over two at (1) and (3) and over three at (2) and (4).

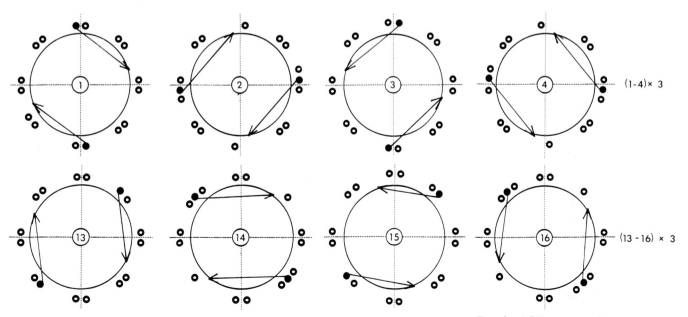

Braid 5: *Oimatsugumi.*

Braid 5. This complex braid has an outside lattice-pattern through which one views a tightly worked core. It is a handsome braid and a somewhat unusual one. It is also an appropriate braid with which to close discussion of category I braiding structures as close inspection reveals that it is simply a #1 braid inside another #1 braid.

The braid is composed of two distinct sets of elements which are indicated by ○ and ● in the set-up diagram. The working set creates a #1 braid on the inside while the passive set floats on the outside. After a repeat of three sequences, the sets change roles. The braid is worked on the round stand so working elements pass easily on the inside of the braid allowing the resting elements to float on the outside.

The braid is usually worked in one color as the color would reverse every three sequences if the two sets were different colors.

(*Oimatsugumi* — old pine tree braid.)

An interesting variation of this braid allows for sets of different colors, one color on the inside and one on the outside. Set 1, the set that, in this variation, consistently works the inside braid, is worked in an identical fashion to the working set in Braid 5. Set 2, however, simply passes through the core of the braid after every three sequences of set 1. The sequence for set 2 is identical to steps 1-4 of Braid 10.

(*Tsukushigumi* — wild horsetail (shoot) braid.)

CATEGORY II: Movement through the core with one or more sets of elements which twine around each other as they pass through the center.

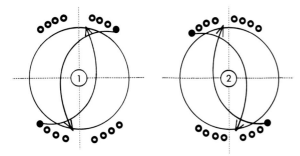

Braid 6: *Hirakakugumi.*

Braid 6. This is a very simple braid to make. However, as in all round stand braids, it is important to move the elements *up and over the center* and to twine them exactly over the middle of the stand. *Hirakakugumi* is a loose braid which becomes weak and messy if it is worked carelessly.

Figure 5 shows three different color set-ups: (1) chevron patterns, (2) horizontal bands, and (3) vertical stripes.

(*Hirakakugumi* — flat, square braid.)

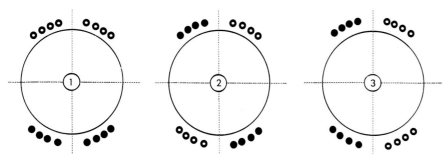

Figure 5. Color charts for Braid 6: *Hirakakugumi.*

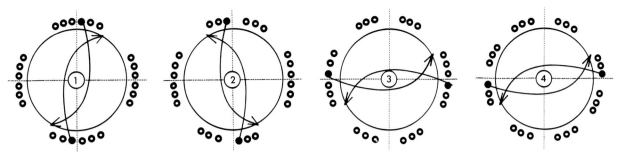

Braid 7: *Marugenji.*

Braid 7. The movements in this braid are obviously very closely related to Braid 6 as diagonal opposites twine through the core of the braid. However, movement now is from center-out instead of from outside-in and a second, horizontal, set of elements has been added. These changes make a round instead of a square cross section. Actually, *Marugenji* is not a round braid in the sense that most category I braids are round. Rather it is an eight-faced braid, but the 45° angle between faces is softened considerably by the many tiny filaments of silk in each element which make the braid appear quite round. It is firmer and more tightly constructed than Braid 6.

(*Marugenjigumi* — (Prince) Genji's round braid.)

Marugenji, although it has not always been known by that name, is an old braid and a very fine one. It is worked somewhat differently by different braiding houses. Braid 7 is from Kyoto. Braid 8, which eliminates the center twine, is from Tokyo.

CATEGORY III: Movement through the core with two distinct sets of elements set at right angles to each other and with no movement between the sets.

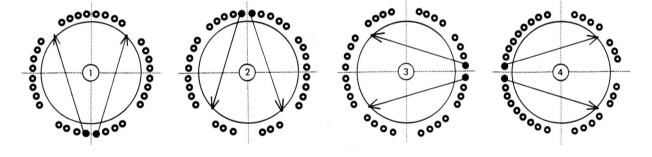

Braid 8: *Marugenji.*

A: Sets have identical movements.
Braid 8. In this version of *Marugenji*, elements move directly through the core of the braid with no center twine. Each group of four produces one of the eight faces of the braid. As the direction of the diagonal slant of the elements alternates from face to face, adjoining faces have opposite slants and appear as chevrons when the braid is worked in more than one color. The length of the chevrons is determined by the number of elements in each ⅛ section. Handsome in two colors, *Marugenji* is also very effective when worked with 'bokashi', or color gradation.

Figure 7 shows three different color set-ups: (1) four-element dark and light chevrons alternating both vertically and horizontally; (2) two-element dark and light chevrons alternating vertically but not horizontally. In other words,

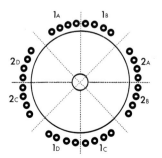

Figure 6. Diagram of 8 faces of Braid 8, *Marugenji.*

a two-element dark zigzag is followed, vertically, by a two-element light zigzag around the braid. And (3) eight-element chevrons graduated from dark to light as follows: 4, 3, 2, 1.

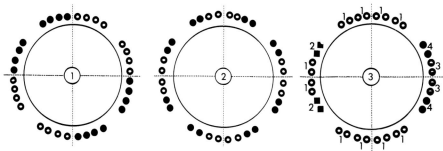

Figure 7. Color charts for Braid 8, *Marugenji.*

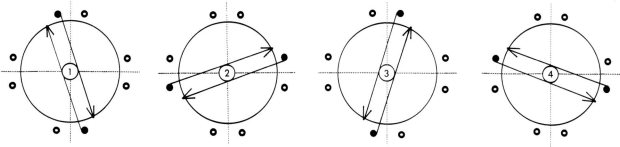

Braid 9: *Kyoyatsu.*

Braid 9. In this 'eight-element braid from Kyoto', pairs of opposite elements change position through the core of the braid.

Kyoyatsu is a gentler, looser braid than its cousin, the 'eight-element braid from Edo' (Braid 1). It would be quite inappropriate for the armor and fastenings that *Edoyatsu* and its multi-element category I cousins serve so well.

(*Kyoyatsu* — eight-element (braid) from Kyoto.)

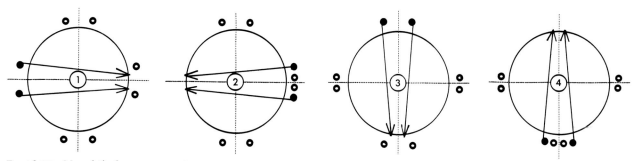

Braid 10: *Narabikakuyatsugumi.*

Braid 10. This little braid, though quite loosely constructed, is gentle and pleasing. As each element passes directly through the core, it stays balanced and centered.

The simple movement of elements from one side to the inside of the opposite pair is one that is used often in braids of the III B type in which one set can be perceived as 'warp' and the other set as 'weft'. Additional elements can be added in which case the working elements move from the outside of one side to the center of the other and back in the same fashion.

(*Narabikakuyatsugumi* — paired, square eight-element braid.)

B: Sets have different movements.

These braids are distinguished by distinct center and border elements which are worked separately and differently and which appear as distinct units in the finished braid. To illustrate the category, I will diagram one of a series of braids which are known, for somewhat obscure reasons, as (Prince) Genji's braids. In d'Harcourt's terminology these structures would be classified as 'plaiting-weaving' as they can be understood to have both a 'warp' (the set at the 'top' and 'bottom' of the stand) and a 'weft' (the horizontal set). The Genji braids can become quite complex but the principle remains the same — an even number of 'warps' (set 1) resting in an 'open shed' position and 'changing shed' after the insertion of the 'weft' elements (set 2). In some Genji braids the centers are moved first, in others the edges.

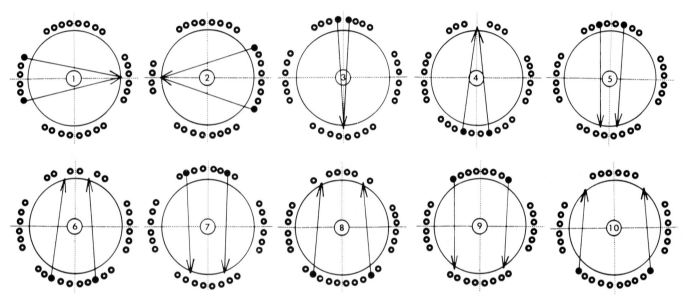

Braid 11: *Genjigumi.*

Braid 11. This is a fairly typical Genji braid. It is not necessary to use three double pairs of 'wefts' but the tiny chevron-patterned edges they produce are both clean and elegant.

All 'weft pairs' must be tensioned (lifted and pulled) after each sequence until the braid is completely 'warp-faced'. To prepare for the following sequence, a small space is then opened at the center of the sides and front of the stand to accommodate the entry of paired elements in steps 1-3. Too large a gap causes loose, uneven braiding.

Color can be used to add interest to a Genji braid. The center (set 1) and border (set 2) may be of contrasting colors and either set may be composed of more than one color. Adding a color to double pairs in set 1 creates 'warp-way' stripes while an extra color in set 2 livens the chevron design on the edges.

Of particular design interest is the Genji braid's potential to show off a variety of 'warp-float' patterns. To work such patterns, the braider simply leaves unworked the 'warp' elements he desires to float for as many sequences as the pattern demands and practical considerations permit (see Photo 12).

CATEGORY IV: Movement through the core with two sets of elements and with movement between the sets. (In the course of the braiding, elements move from one set to the other changing role from 'warp' to 'weft' as they do so.)

The type of oblique interlacement of elements that is characteristic of this category is commonly called plaiting and produces comparatively wide, flat, flexible structures.

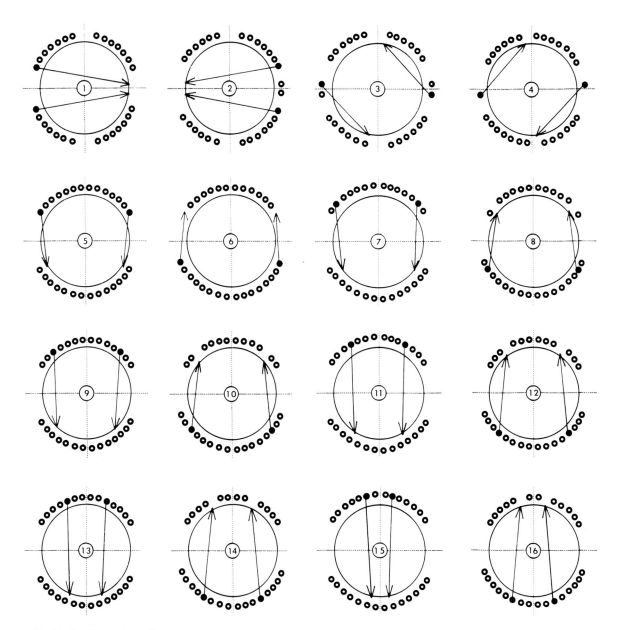

Braid 12: *Koamigumi.*

Braid 12. This is a simple but characteristic plait and is shown here to demonstrate how plaiting is done on a round stand within the context of the Japanese braiding tradition.

(*Koamigumi* — little plaited braid.)

Koamigumi is a cousin to the time-honored *karagumi* (old Chinese braid) which has a somewhat more complex weft arrangement and which reverses design at mid-point to form distinctive diamond patterns on its firm, flat surface. Wider and more complex plaits than these are generally worked on the high stand.

CATEGORY V: Combination braids.

There are a few braids which do not fit neatly into any of the above four categories. Most of these, such as *Tsukushigumi* (discussed as a Braid 5 variation), have one (or more) set in one category and another (or others) in a second. A very few seem to be on the borderline between two categories. Braid 9, *Kyoyatsu*, comfortably fits into category III, movement through the core, and yet it can also be seen as a logical extension of Braids 1 and 2 in category I, movement around the core. Such braids, however, are an exception and the four categories outlined above would seem, on the whole, to provide a useful method of organizing the wide range of braids in this varied and rich tradition.

Conclusion

This paper has attempted to provide an introduction to the basic constructions of Japanese braids as they are done on the round and the square stands. Once a structure is understood, it can be worked quickly and easily. The movement of its elements forms certain distinct patterns that, with experience, becomes predictable and, with practice, almost second-nature to the braider. In a way, these movements are like the most fundamental steps in a folk-dance tradition, a few basic repeatable movements which can be put together into a small series of interactions which, in turn, can be choreographed into a wonderful complexity of distinct folk dances. In another idiom they are like the epithets Albert Lord describes in *The Singer of Tales*, those set, stock phrases with which a skilled ballad-singer is able to touch the full range of his audience's terrors, passions and aspirations and lead it, with him, over the 'wine-dark sea' on the spiritual odyssey of his hero.

Much remains to be written about Japanese braids. The 8th century Shoso-in collection of Chinese braiding from the height of the expansive T'ang Dynasty represents the foundation on which the Japanese tradition developed. While many of the braids in this collection appear to have been worked on stands similar to the round and square stands in use today and with construction methods that would feel familiar to a modern Japanese braider, some, quite definitely, were not. The Shoso-in braids deserve special attention. Little appears to be known, as yet, about subsidiary working methods such as that illustrated in the Muromachi period scroll painting, *Nanajuichiban Shokunin Uta Awase no E* and depicted in Photo 7. Little is known, for that matter, about the history and development of the main stands in use today, particularly the *taka-dai* and the *ayatake-dai* with their related, but quite distinct, working methods.

This paper has presented a representative sample of the wealth of contemporary round and square stand braids and a discussion of the principles which guide the braider as he uses them to re-create time-honored favorites and to explore new variations. I hope that it will provide a basis for further research in the history and techniques of Japanese braiding and that it might serve to open discussion with braiders and scholars working in other traditions in which one finds different axes of interrelationships between structure and tool and technique, different ways of thinking and of working the braids.

BIBLIOGRAPHY

Many books on braiding have been published in the last few years in Japan. Following is a list of some of the best.

Domyo, Shinbe-e. *Himo*. Tokyo: Gakuseisha, 1963.
    Written by the head of the famous braiding house of the same name, this book is a good general history of braiding in Japan.
Ota, Tosaburo, Kojiro Suganuma and Kaoru Yamaki. *Kumihimo*. Otsu: Minzokubunka Kenkyukai, 1969.
    This is probably the most scholarly and comprehensive treatment of the subject.

Shoso-in Office, ed. *Shoso-in no Kumihimo*. Tokyo: Heibonsha, 1973.
> Researched by Issei Yamaoka and put out by the Shoso-in Office of the Imperial Household Agency, this lovely book includes many good plates of braids in the Shoso-in collection and current research on them.

Yamaoka, Kazunari. *Domyo no Kumihimo*. Tokyo: Shufunotomo, 1975.

-----. *Dento no Kumihimo*. Tokyo: Shufunotomo, 1976.
> These two books were written under the auspices of the Domyo braiding house and are among the best of the 'how-to' books.

Following is a list of publications in English. While not of the scope of the books listed above, they provide an introduction to the subject and working diagrams of some of the braids.

Foster, Mary Sue and Charlotte Loveland. *Kumihemo* [sic]. Wichita: self-published, 1977.
> Written for use in the art education department of Wichita State University, this nice little publication was the result of a single visit to a braiding workshop and a few materials collected on a trip to Japan by Foster.

Kinoshita, Masa. "Kumihimo: An Ancient Japanese Bobbin Braid", *Shuttle, Spindle and Dyepot*, Winter 1977, #3 and Summer 1980, #43.
> Masa Kinoshita, writer and textile artist, has probably done the most work on Japanese braiding techniques of the authors listed here.

Kliot, Jules and Kaethe. *Kumi Himo, Techniques of Japanese Plaiting*. Berkeley: Some Place, 1977.
> The Kliot booklet contains instructions for a beginning American braider and includes working diagrams for 14 braids including some of the most important and versatile of the old braids.

Speiser, Noémi. "The Japanese Art of Braiding", *CIBA Review*, 1974/4.

-----. "The Techniques and the Methods of Braiding, A Technological Research in Progress", *CIETA Bulletin #46*, 1977.
> Speiser brings to her work a thorough understanding of the nature of braids and braiding and a knowledge of several quite diverse braiding traditions.

IN SEARCH OF "COLLAPSE"*

BY LILLIAN ELLIOTT

Some years ago Anne Blinks showed me several textiles she had woven in which an odd thing happened. The handspun yarns which had been rather tightly spun relaxed when the cloth was removed from the loom and washed. In the process a pattern formed which resembled a loom controlled herringbone despite the fact that the cloth was woven in tabby. The pattern seemed slightly erratic and would disappear in areas. Anne dubbed this effect "collapse". She was uncertain about whether this "surface pattern" formed only in handwoven textiles made with handspun yarns. Although Anne did not completely understand the process, she was sure of several ingredients for it to happen: some of the yarns had to be overspun, and the spacing in the reed had to be open enough so that later in the washing, the yarns would have the room to move about and regroup.

This idea was an intriguing one to me, but I was too occupied with other things to do anything about it then. Several years passed before I had occasion to remember those textiles. In 1970 I was given some cotton yarn so overspun that it was difficult to reel off in winding a warp. I persevered, however, and when I saw my resulting bumpy cloth I was amazed at how much it reminded me of Peruvian textiles in feel and pebbly surface. At the same time it called to mind Anne's earlier wool collapsed cloth. Collapse seemed to be a worthwhile direction to pursue since I was pleased at the surface I had inadvertently achieved with the overspun yarn. "Overspin and open space" became my theme as I attempted to understand and use the process of collapse. I continued to use Anne's term to describe that process. This paper is a brief general recounting of what I've learned in those investigations.

In order to achieve any real collapse, some yarns used must be more overspun than others. It seems that there is a ratio between the thickness of the yarn, the amount of spin present, and the density of the sett. Any overspun yarn has its own ratio of spacing to bring out its optimum collapse pattern. The overspin can be in warp, weft, or in both directions. The amount and direction of spin determines the surface patterns by setting up a tension which shifts the yarns and changes the spaces formed between the yarns, the interstices, when the yarn relaxes in washing. During the weaving the cloth appears to be a taut, flat, open spaced textile.

Actually, there are two distinct varieties of collapse. Sometimes, the cloth simply crimps back on itself in irregular folds and becomes quite elastic, occasionally, ridiculously so. Other times, it forms distinct diamonds or "tracks". In both varieties there is extreme drawing in of the cloth in at least one direction. It is not true shrinkage since the cloth can usually be stretched back under tension to near the full pre-washing width, and temporarily held there. When released it will resume its now natural crimped state. Occasionally, both varieties are present in one cloth.

In the "diamond" variety of collapse small indentations are formed on the surface. They make diamond shapes, or sometimes small surface line patterns called "hen tracks" by Anne and "crow's foot" by industry. Today in industry a

Warps run vertically in the photographs.

Photo 1. Example of tracking or diamond pattern, wool.

*With a grateful nod to John Irwin.

large machine called the "crab", whose purpose is to set the weave, is used to pull out those random marks which sometimes appear in cloth, particularly visible when the cloth is woven in white wool in tabby structure. There apparently were, and perhaps still are, great community get-togethers in Scotland which were called "crabbing bees" at which everyone seated around a large table tugged at a newly woven blanket until all those random marks were pulled out of the cloth. After a great deal of tugging accompanied by singing, the cloth would have a smooth surface.* One is, of course, reminded of that other great textile social event in this country, the quilting bee.

I, perverse as I am, get great pleasure from the notion of taking what is perceived to be a disadvantage, and by exaggeration transforming it into an element of positive value.

My work in collapse has been done entirely with commercial yarns. I have sometimes had more twist added to the commercial yarn, and have had some yarns plied together for particular effects. To my delight the process seems to work as clearly with commercial yarns as with handspun. The results are larger in scale and therefore more obvious than in Anne's handspun pieces, but they have the same characteristics: the great elasticity, the irregular deflected surface, and sometimes the diamonds, which appear to be more or less pointed depending on the amount of twist or ply in the yarn. A current T.V. advertisement in praising a brand of English muffins provides us with a description of collapse by speaking of "those wonderful nooks and crannies".

A major problem is in finding appropriate yarns. Some yarns appear to be overspun, but when washed the spin softens and disappears, and no collapse is effected. When overtwisted yarns are available they are most often in the finest thread count, which limits scale and makes it difficult to do large-scale weavings. Most yarns seem to be balanced out to make them easier to use. Usually, they are plied together in the opposite direction from the spin to neutralize it. Perhaps, worst of all, the fiber content is frequently unspecified which makes it harder to plan for collapse. Synthetics are sometimes added for reasons of cost, ease of handling, or eventual care. That poses a problem, since none of the synthetics I have worked with, no matter how overspun they appeared to be, retained that character in woven cloth. In the absence of over-spun yarns, overplied yarns will sometimes substitute, although the results are generally not as remarkable. Collapse can be achieved with both single and plied yarns.

Overspun yarns tend to tangle. They double back on themselves making it awkward at least, sometimes near impossible to manage them. Extreme over-spinning gives the weaver extreme difficulties. However, I found it worthwhile to persist because the energy and resilience of the yarn is somehow captured in the finished cloth.

I was most successful working with cotton, and reasonably successful with wool. I felt extremely limited with the silk yarns on the market. In this country virtually all the silk available is spun silk, not reeled (continuous filament) silk. Despite all my efforts adding twist to the spun silk I was unable to add enough spin to achieve any real collapse. In crepe production twist is added to filament silk as part of the "throwing" operation just after reeling. I tried a few samples with the limited amount of Japanese crepe-twist (reeled) silk available to me. Although the yarn was highly twisted, the scale was minute and not nearly as dramatic as what I was able to achieve in other materials.

When I first embarked on this project I found myself totally disregarding color, and trying to concentrate on spin. I strained my eyes checking the amount and direction of twist. I searched for yarns which tangled. I asked for yarns others had given up on. I tested yarns to see which ones doubled back on

*Crabbing is not to be confused with another finishing process, fulling, which is sometimes accomplished by a group of people. Fulling permanently shrinks and thickens the cloth. There is an illustration in *National Geographic Magazine,* July 1952, p. 103 of the fulling process, which shows Portnalong women as they "waulk (Scottish: shrink) the tweed" to the rhythm of Gaelic songs.

Photo 2. Mohair and wool collapse.

Photo 3. Alpaca collapse woven by Anne Blinks, spinning by Macia Friedman. Based on a Peruvian loin cloth in the collection at the DeYoung Museum, San Francisco. *Photo by Pat Hickman.*

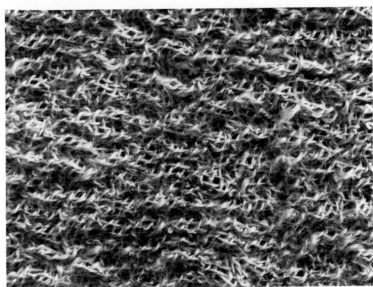

Photo 4. Linen warp and linen and wool weft collapse.

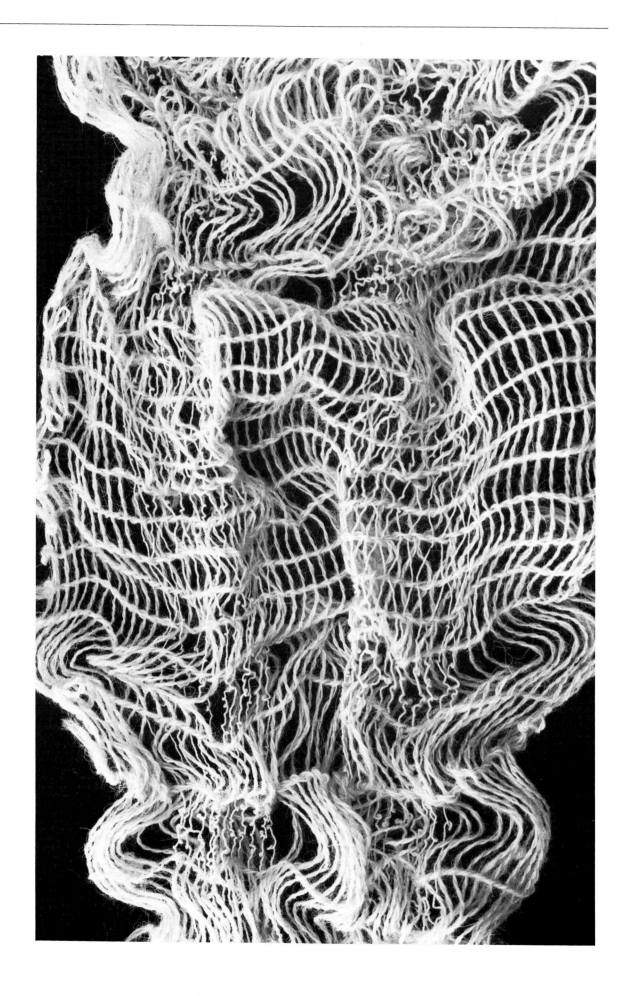

Photo 5. Twining sample with over-spun wool, woven by Nora Rogers. *Photo by Nora Rogers.*

themselves. Later, I learned to ask for pure fibers so I could begin to anticipate my results. Eventually, to my great pleasure I found I had learned to recognize overspun yarn by touch.

Yarns need not be extremely overspun, though the spin must be pronounced. When direction of spin is the key factor, many other possibilities are available. Direction of spin can be alternated in warp, weft, or both. Warp can be spun in one direction, weft in the other. Beautiful collapse patterns can be formed working with directional spin, although the tracking patterns occur less often than with pronounced overspin itself.

Most of the weaving which I did was in tabby, but I did try some twill samples which were unlike any other twills I've seen. If the yarn is left floating free on the surface as in twill weaves, and the yarn is overspun, individual strands will curl back on themselves, and become an important factor in the surface appearance. Many of the ancient Peruvian gauze weaves show this overspun characteristic as much as they show varieties of open weave structure. In tabby, because there are so many intersections, the yarn is held down and the whole cloth shifts within itself, forming collapse patterns. Somehow, for me most of the fun seemed to be in using the simplest cloth structure possible, plain weave (tabby), and then just watching the yarn unfold its individual hidden pattern within the cloth.

It is possible to achieve collapse using other weaves. On page 183 in *Elements of Weaving* by Azalea Thorpe and Jack Larsen there is a photograph and a reference to an accordian pleated dress fabric made of dupione or spun silk warp and fine worsted weft in herringbone threading woven by Mariel Collins. This is a fine example of collapse. Nora Rogers used highly overspun yarn in twining samples. Interesting results were achieved because the individual threads left free moved individually in a way related to my twill samples.

Crepe can be achieved with chemical treatment. I have tried some chemical experiments on silk without much success. Cotton is treated with caustic soda to produce plissés and blister crepes, which are cousins to collapse. Seersuckers, often linked with plissés, are produced by using slack tension on parts of the warp. Caustic soda is the chief ingredient in mercerizing, a process which consists of immersing cotton in caustic soda solutions, and washing and drying it under tension. When tension is absent in that process, cotton shrinks significantly. Mercerization permanently strengthens the cotton fiber and increases both luster and dyeing affinity. In reading about silk and crepe caustic soda is always mentioned, saying that it is unfortunate that the latter dissolves silk, and that it would be desirable to find a single ingredient that affects silk as caustic soda does cotton. In *Fiberarts* magazine (Nov./Dec. 1980) there is an interesting article which describes the use of caustic soda on silk for extreme surface effects. This suggests many related possibilities.

In 1973 as I first became excited about collapse I was teaching a weaving class at the University of California, Berkeley, and I gave that problem as an assignment. Many students began by weaving textiles composed of materials which by nature behave very differently from one another, most often using wool and linen together. We all know those materials "give" quite differently, and shrink differently from one another. Some of the results were successful. Usually, they were difficult to weave because of tension problems. The next major direction, especially for those students comfortable with spinning, was to overspin all their yarns. Those results were not so predictable. Everything was so overspun that nothing happened.

I once heard Josef Albers give a public lecture. His rather simplistic message (at the risk of heresy) was that colors affect their neighbors. The audience was composed of visual people who were already aware of that. My message is, I suppose, as simplistic: the spin of yarns affects their neighboring yarns. Weavers, I think are not so aware of that. It's a rather simple story, but with infinitely complex possibilities. If yarns are so close together that they cannot shift about, no collapse occurs. If, on the other hand there is moving space, the yarns shift, regroup, and form patterns on their own, dependent on the amount and direction of individual spin. It's hard to keep the metaphor of crowded urban life out of mind.

There is no term corresponding to collapse in the textile literature. A student interested in work I had shown him once asked where he could read about it. No description of this process appears in any of the standard reference books. This seems odd to me when I find the procedure so fascinating and the results so worthwhile. The closest thing referred to in the books is under the term "crepe". However, there are many varieties of crepe, including those achieved by weave structure, chemical treatments, and different warp tensions, as well as those created by overspinning and the use of directional spinning (our old friends in achieving collapse). Technically, I suppose, collapse could be called one variety of crepe. It shares with crepe an interesting deflected surface and a beautiful "feel" or "hand". However, the collapse which can be done in handweaving is generally so much larger in scale that it appears to be quite a different phenomenon from the very subtle silk Chinese or Japanese crepes, usually achieved with directional spin, that most of us have in mind when we think of crepe. Since everything is magnified in close-up photography, it is difficult to be aware of major differences in scale from photographic details. There is an equalizing effect in photography, but the actual textiles are worlds apart.

Photo 6. "Ribbon Candy", collapse using space-dyed synthetics and natural brown cotton, 16" × 16". (*Collection of Sarah Redfield*)

Photo 7. Mohair and wool collapse.

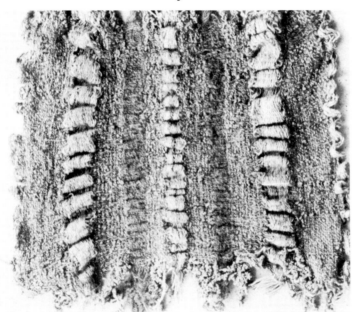
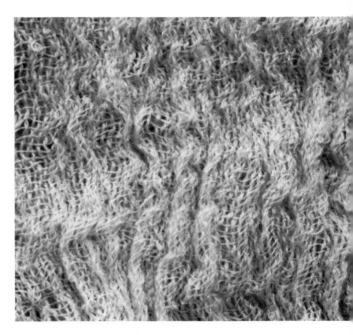

There are historical precedents. The most extreme seem to be heavily collapsed Turkish silk shirts used by both men and women as undergarments. I was first made aware of the Turkish use of silk in those shirts by Pat Hickman who was in a weaving class of mine at U.C. Berkeley when I used collapse as one teaching assignment. At that time she was guest curating an exhibit of Turkish everyday textiles at the Lowie Museum of Anthropology at U.C. Berkeley. Pat was struggling to get satisfactory results in her own efforts at weaving collapse when she phoned me in great excitement to tell me of shirts she had seen in gathering materials for the Lowie Museum exhibit. Since then both of us have seen many of those wonderful shirts, some still not quite finished. The shirts traditionally have been an important part of the dowry. Our research on those shirts is ongoing, and there are still many unanswered questions.

There are also similar textiles from Greece, full gathered pants and shirts which are collapsed. Today, there are collapsed cotton shirts from Turkey and Greece, although they are not the equals of the old harsh beautiful silk ones. In this country for the past several years there have been cotton fabrics on the market from India with an all-over collapse pattern.

I have found that it is not necessary to use overspun yarns throughout one piece. More interesting and effective collapse occurs if the overspun yarns are spaced within the work. When I felt that I had some control over what I was doing, I realized how few overspun yarns were necessary in order to end with collapse. I decided to combine overspun yarns with metallic yarns, since the metallics are the least flexible and elastic of all yarns, and I felt that they would be the most difficult to move into collapse patterns. I used grossly overspun cotton yarns spaced one per inch in a lustrous rayon warp. The weft was primarily a metallic one with bands of cotton in sections. I was quite surprised to see the resulting strong collapse pattern.

Once aware of collapse, I feel that it changes the weaver's view. It reminds me of my change in geographical surroundings, so that the flat Michigan environs where I grew up seem very dull to me now that I have grown accustomed to the hilly terrain of Northern California. The pursuit of the elusive collapse can result in the weaver's becoming more aware of individual fibers, amount of spin, direction of spin, and combinations previously unthought of. Hopefully, the weaver will have increased possibilities as a result of this new awareness. An equal pleasure is that suddenly a wide group of historic textiles will appear in a new light.

Photo 8. Silk dress fabric with background of crepe-de-chine (plain weave woven with dense silk warp and crepe twist silk filling alternating 2S-2Z).

Photo 9. Two-ply cotton collapse fabric.

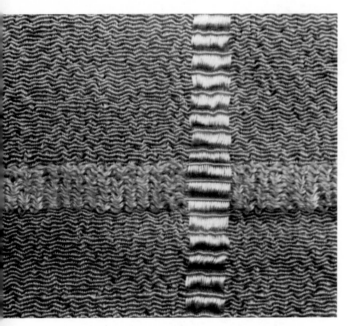

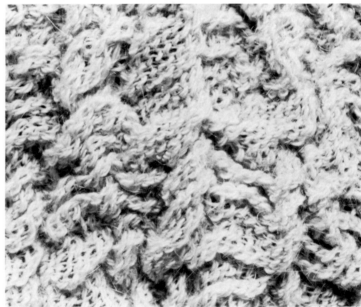

BIBLIOGRAPHY

Bissell, June. "Caustic Soda". *Fiberarts*, vol. 7, no. 6, Nov./Dec. 1980, pp. 43-46.

Denny, Grace G. *Fabrics and How to Know Them*. Philadelphia, London: J.B. Lippincott Co., 1923.

Fairchild's Dictionary of Textiles, ed. Dr. Isabel B. Wingate. New York: Fairchild Publications, Inc., 1959, 3rd printing 1974.

Irwin, John. "Journey in Search of Ikats". *Quarterly Journal of the Guilds of Weavers, Spinners, and Dyers*, no. 47, Sept. 1963. Brighton, Sussex.

Matthews' Textile Fibers. 5th edition, ed. Herbert R. Mauersberger. New York: John Wiley and Sons, Inc., 1947.

National Geographic Magazine. illustration, Portnalong women "Waulk the tweed". July 1952, p. 103.

Thorpe, Azalea S. and Jack Larsen. *Elements of Weaving*. Garden City, New York: Doubleday and Co., Inc., 1967.

Woolman, Mary Schenck and Ellen Beers McGowan. *Textiles*. New York: MacMillan Co., 1922.

The Wool Bureau, Inc., the United States Branch of the International Wool Secretariat has its Technical Services Center at 225 Crossways Park Drive, Woodbury, Long Island, New York 11797. They will help with specific problems.

Editor's Note: Handspinners might be interested in some specific guidelines for spinning to achieve collapse by Bette Hochberg, "Add a New Twist to Your Spinning," in *Spin·Off*, Interweave Press: Loveland, Colorado, 1981.

We wanted Anne also to be a part of the monograph. But it did not seem fair to suggest she write a meaty article, with all the labor it would entail. After all, this Festschrift is for *her. Here is her mode for naming sheep, so that you may "meet Anne face-to-face".*

ON THE NAMING OF SHEEP

BY ANNE BLINKS

Sheep have names for obvious reasons like other folk — but the choice is somewhat broader. The social pressures of kinfolk and friends is almost nil, while the demands for familial identification, though desirable, are somewhat less than among humans.

Some are quite obvious. Samson was of course the son of Sam; but Sam himself was named for my late father — since he came to us on my father's birthday, his hundredth to be sure, but still to be remembered. Or Columbia, who was born the day the space ship landed the first time. Or Natividad, who was born on my birthday. Or Soledad, the only child born on the place the year after the great holocaust, when 12 were killed by dogs — including *all* the rams. Obviously her mother was sent to visit. Soledad's daughters were Lupé and Inez, so we would remember whose they were. Soledad took the black Lupé at once; but when the white Inez arrived some hours later, she would have none of her. So Inez became a bottle baby and my constant companion. When my Boxer bitch Maria died, I was bemoaning my grief when a friend called my attention to the white fluff underfoot and said "Towser" there would have to do for a puppy. So Inez is now Towser. Maria, of course, was named for a favorite aunt. Lupé, a pretty little dark thing, was so called because she looked very like a local radio announcer so named. She doesn't now.

Some have only numbers (though all have numbers, too) or a fugitive name that vanishes when some incident occurs to make some other name more pertinent. Like The Coot who took refuge in the Goose Pond when the dogs came one moonlit night. Everybody else had run to the barn, but one was missing — a dark shape immobile in dark mud and water up to her waist. My husband brashly said he would rescue her; but he, too, got stuck fast in the black goo. She wouldn't or couldn't budge. So I got planks and made a ramp and got a rope which he tied onto her neck. And then he pushed, while I held on to the rope and leaned back with all 200 pounds of me. With a great sucking swoosh she scrambled ashore, seemingly none the worse, but very wet and dirty. Since she was big with lamb and very near term, I was worried that she would deliver then and there, in mud and wet and darkness. So I hurried her to the shed to be wiped and dried off at least — leaving my husband to scramble out on his own (on the plank). As I was reproached for abandoning him I explained, "Well, *you* are not pregnant." After all this, the lady was named The Coot (sounded better than Mud Hen).

She had two sisters, also named when grown. Trinidad, for her habit of producing triplets. She had three sets of them plus a set of twins. The other, William Henry Perkin, after the English discoverer of the early synthetic dye, mauve. I wanted my spinning class to remember him and she *was* a weird color, more purple than brown; but I am afraid *not* mauve!

Then on one unfortunate occasion — only once, Candy Crockett to the contrary notwithstanding — a ewe went down with "lambing paralysis" just days before she was due. (Bad management on my part.) So the vet proceeded with a Caesarean and produced from her smoking side first one live lamb very sharp and lively, and then, after a few minutes a second who took some time to breathe and come around — quite flat. So they were named Sharp and Flat. Both grew up strong and active with definite and different personalities. Their mother never woke up, so they were bottle babies brought up by the Boxer Maria, and did as she did — racing 'round and 'round the pond, sometimes leading, sometimes chasing, but jumping over box hurdles put there for sport. Sometimes they would be joined by all the other lambs on the place, to their mothers' horror. Since Maria chased squirrels, they chased squirrels too, though never caught one as far as I know. Caused some comment.

Many pairs of twins, the usual thing, were named for some circumstance of their birth or their color. As Pasquale, born on Easter, and his sister Selena who appeared just as the full moon was rising. Or Maximus and Minima, a pair of unequal size. Or Anthracite and Dolomite, another pair of one black and one white. Or Viola and Sebastian, born on "Twelfth Night". Or another pair born of a very adoring young ewe, so Mother's Pride and Mother's Joy. Then, of course, a very pretty pair of whites, Flora and Dora. Flora was the handsomest; she died young. But Dora had the best fleece and produced lamb after lamb, usually in pairs — Dolly, DeeDee, Dugal, Doreen, Dotty, etc., etc. Some are named for months — especially if it is not a usual month for lambing — Augustus, September, Janus.

All the girls this year are "A's": Allison, Asenath, Abigail — a rather stupid idea, but I can at least remember how old they are. After they were well named there came the three little white Cheviots — adopted. They are seemingly identical; but on closer examination one has pure white ears — so Blanche; one a dark spot on the right ear — Dextra; and one a larger spot on the left — Sinestra. I am betting those two are heterozygous and may have black lambs. That's not all, but these are the latest. Enough.

That was enough until this morning. Now Soledad, after two years on the bench, has surprised us with a pair of black twins. Maybe Ebony and Jet? Or should it be Possibly Max and Probably Max? (The father is in some doubt.)

BREEDING SHEEP FOR COLORED WOOL

BY JOANNE NISSEN

Interest in naturally colored wool has risen dramatically with the revival of home spinning and weaving skills. Many spinners have a small pasture in which they have begun to establish flocks of colored sheep. Others have recognized a ready market for these colored wools and have begun commercial-size flocks either in conjunction with existing white flocks or as a separate farm enterprise. Some flocks originated with spinners who wanted to control the entire process by developing their own preferred wool characteristics, as well as increased quality and cleanliness. There now exist flocks of black, brown, grey and vari-colored sheep from which the spinner may choose.

With this increased interest in handspinning and weaving, attention is focused on the colored fleece to achieve a range of colors not available with dyed wool. Color has been introduced from mutton breeds, but the concentration in sheep breeds is currently on the wool or dual purpose breeds to achieve a superior fleece for the handspinner. No single breed is dominating the popularity, as the ultimate use of spun wool varies from baby clothes or garments worn next to the skin to extremely durable rugs and unique wall hangings. The type of wool to complement these projects ranges from the finest grades to the coarsest.

Black or brown color in naturally pigmented wool is the result of the presence of granules of "melanin", a pigment which is produced by a special kind of cell called a "melanocyte". These cells are colored themselves. In colored skin they are distributed between the cells of the basal layer of the epidermis and among presumptive fiber cells in the follicle bulb (Henderson).

The function of color in sheep is not certain, although it must be assumed to have given the animal protection by providing camouflage. The darker color would have blended in with the background and the pale bellies would have helped neutralize the shadow formed under the belly (Ryder and Stephenson). Some of the Bighorns living in snow country in Alaska are completely white.

It must be noted that fleece color does not always have a genetic basis. It is known that certain bacteria can cause blue, pink or green coloration, and fleeces that are constantly wet in warm weather may be stained yellow. Black fleeces are subject to color change with loss of color on the tips due to sun bleaching. Sun bleaching varies greatly with the individual, and there may be even further bleaching down through the fiber or in certain areas as on the back where the locks may part exposing more of the fiber area to the sun. In addition, as some animals age, color may be lost from the fleece. A deficiency in copper or zinc will cause a reduction in pigmentation because the melanin is produced in lesser quantities (Blair). Consequently fleece color in wool breeds can be described only at birth before environmental factors enter the picture. Because of the non-genetic factors, the wide range of colors and patterns within pigmented fleeces can be almost unlimited.

The generally accepted genetically controlled colors and patterns found at birth in sheep considered colored are: black, brown, agouti, skimlet (grey or roan), badger face, reverse badger face (mouflon pattern), piebald (black spots), and self color (white markings on black sheep).

Agouti: known as the wild color, it is a coloration pattern in which there is a paler band below the dark tip of the fiber. It is still found in wild sheep today, and in the hair of the birth coat and extremities of some domestic breeds. It is also the coloration pattern found in many species of wild animals throughout the world.

Skimlet (grey or roan): a coat having a mixture of white and pigmented fibers. Grey is the result of black and white, and the roan the result of red and white. The inheritance of this coat is still uncertain.

Badger face: sharp change from pigmented to lightly- or non-pigmented wool on moving from the belly to the flank and side. Other features seen are black legs and a black bar over each eye, while the lower jaw and the inside of the ears are darker. This pattern may also be known as grelut or gromet.

Reverse badger face (mouflon pattern): sharp change from non-pigmented wool to pigmented wool on moving from the belly to the flank and side. Other commonly seen features are a brownish yellow bar over each eye with the lower jaw and the inside of the ears lighter in color.

Piebald (black spots): the black areas are not symmetrically distributed on each side of the body. They may vary in size and are usually rounded in shape. This pattern is apparently caused by a heredity character that restricts the area of colored wool on the body (Ryder).

Self color (white markings on black sheep): no sharp change in the degree of pigmentation on moving from belly to the flank and side. Commonly has patches of grey or white wool.

Some authorities group piebald and self color into one pattern group and merely state that the amount of pigmented and non-pigmented wool will vary. However, it is seen in the Jacob breed and others referred to as piebald, that the black wool is often longer, straighter and coarser than the white (Ryder). Yet in other breeds the self color pattern will yield a fleece in which both the white and colored wool will have the same count, handle and length, and consequently may be of special interest to the handspinner.

Producing black sheep would be an easy job if they regularly occurred as the result of mating two black parents. However, since black can be the result of either a recessive or dominant gene, depending on the breeds used in the cross, black is not always a predictable result. For instance it is possible for black lambs to be the offspring of two white parents if the parents are carrying recessive black genes. Black is not present in the parents as it is not expressed in the presence of the dominant white gene. Also it is possible for the reverse badger face pattern to be produced by white parents if that recessive pattern is hidden in both parents by the dominant white trait. If one parent is carrying the reverse badger face pattern and the other a recessive black gene, the pattern will express itself as it is the dominant trait of the two.

In addition, it is known that certain color shades are influenced by unidentified modifying genes. Studies are currently being done by geneticists in an attempt to uncover the mysteries of colored sheep. Flock owners are closely watching their breeding programs in an attempt to understand the traits in their own animals.

It is possible to consider color genes to be visible marker genes in the study of domestication and migration of sheep. Sheep were bred for whiteness early in the domestication process, so it is no surprise that white is the common color. The color genes are now found in the relic breeds of isolated areas in Europe: Iceland, Scandinavia, Corsica, some Alpine valleys, and the sandy heaths of the Netherlands and Northern Germany. These breeds also contain a variety of fiber types with the amount of hair and wool varying.

Apparently a few breeds, especially the descendants of the mouflon stock brought to northern Europe by Stone Age migrants, were not selected for whiteness as diligently as the more southern breeds. Consequently such breeds as the Romanov, Finnsheep, the Icelandic sheep, breeds of the British islands of Orkneys, Shetlands, Isle of Man, Outer Hebrides and the St. Kilda group

Figure 1. Badger face.

Figure 2. Reverse badger face.

Figure 3. Piebald.

Figure 4. Self color.

and elsewhere in the north, are found to have more colored individuals. This is also true to a lesser extent for the coarse, long wooled mountain breeds of sheep, with black and color appearing in North Country Cheviots, Lincoln and the various long wooled Scottish breeds.

The fewest black and colored genes seem to be in the descendants of the Spanish Merino. This is no surprise when you realize that the ancestors of the Merino were already bred for whiteness in Mesopotamia at least 4,000 years ago.

Black sheep are still a novelty and therefore draw much attention. They have been used for years in the commercial range flocks in the West as "markers" or counter sheep for each 100 head of white sheep. Additionally in the snow country, black sheep aid in finding a flock after a snowfall. Now in the large flocks of colored sheep in New Zealand it is possible to find white sheep being used as markers!

There currently exists in New Zealand, Australia, the United States and the European countries a growing industry in raising colored flocks. These can range from a few animals to flocks in the hundreds. Many marketing ideas are being generated by this new industry as the resurgence in home handicrafts has expanded demand for colored wool.

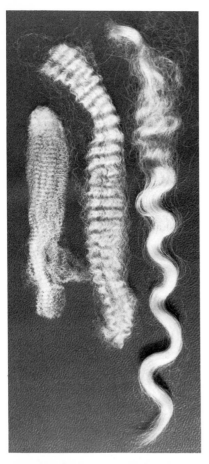

Photo 1. Three examples of crimp in a lock of wool: Short staple, tight crimp, grade 70s, 3 inches. Medium staple, looser crimp, grade 48s, 4½ inches. Long staple, very loose crimp, grade 40s, 6 inches.

Photo 2. Examples of wool from four different breeds found in the United States. Left to right: Karakul, Border Leicester, Columbia, Merino. These show the varying staple length, crimp, and even a hint of the luster. The Karakul is a large fiber and the kemp or hair fibers can be seen, whereas the Merino has a very tight crimp and with the tip showing how soiled a fleece with a high lanolin content can become. *Photos by Mary Harrington*

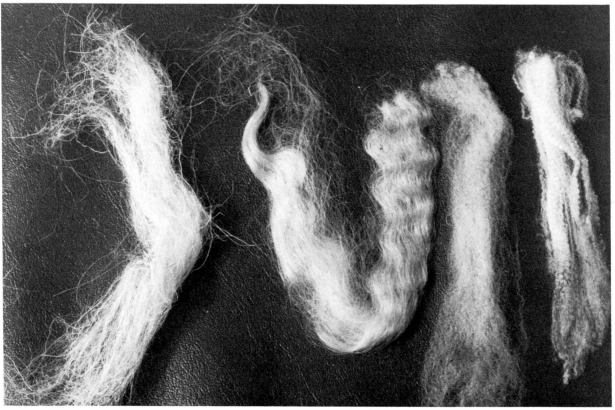

In the United States a coalition of breeders began keeping in touch through the *Black Sheep Newsletter* in the early 1970's. Then in 1977, the Natural Colored Wool Growers Association was formed to serve the needs of these colored wool breeders as well as spinners and weavers. The NCWGA publishes a periodical, *The Marker*, and is currently establishing a registration program for colored sheep throughout the United States. The New Zealand Black and Coloured Sheep Breeders Association was formed in 1978 and is extremely active in that country promoting colored sheep. The South Australian Coloured Sheep Owner's Society, Inc., has been actively helping some colored wool grower groups to process their wool and to market it commercially in various forms both internally and for export.

Flock owners with colored animals vary in their goals. As previously mentioned, some spinners are able to have a few of their own animals and are no doubt attempting to produce the fleece most suitable for the type of yarns they want to work with as to color, grade and handle. Consideration must always be taken with the suitability of breed to climate, but in a small scale operation accommodation can be made to allow a producer an attempt to raise some breeds not typical of their geographical area.

Some producers are trying to have a uniform wool clip in grade if not color, so they can supply an established market with many identical fleeces. This might be typical in New Zealand and Australia where there is a large colored wool clip that is being processed into forms such as sliver and batting as well as remaining as raw fleece and being marketed both internally and for export. On the other hand, many producers such as myself wish to keep some variety of breeds or crossbreds in their flocks so as to show diversity in the fleeces presented to retail stores, thus giving the stores a range in colors, grades, staple lengths, and handle from which they may select fleeces best suited for their retail clientele.

There are also producers that sell directly from their farm or ranch without going through retail stores. They may sell entire fleeces or just a few pounds. Some flock owners even have a day when buyers come out to the farm and choose a fleece while it is still on the animal. Often those buyers come back the day of shearing to collect their choice. Occasionally a spinner will obtain a fleece from an individual animal and in the enthusiasm with that particular fleece will insist on getting that same animal's fleece every year, even though as that animal ages, the fleece color, crimp and handle may change. (Through the years the fleece becomes more open, drier feeling, and loses crimp and handle.)

Finally, it is interesting to note that many of the foundation animals in the California and nearby flocks trace their origin back to a weaver who in her attempt to closely match the color found in ancient textiles, decided she best grow her own! This Festschrift is in honor of that weaver.

BIBLIOGRAPHY

Blair, H.T. Article in *Black Baa.* #9, November 1978.

Ensminger, M.E. *Sheep and Wool Science.* Danville, Illinois: The Interstate Printers and Publishers, Inc., 1970.

Henderson, A.E. *Growing Better Wool.* Australia: A.H. & A.W. Reed, 1968.

Ryder, Michael L. *Sheep and Wool for Handicraft Workers.* Penicuik, Midlothian, Scotland: Pen-y-coe Press, 1978.

----- and S.K. Stephenson. *Wool Growth.* London and New York: Academic Press, 1968.

Spurlock, Glen M. "Inheritance of Coat Color in Sheep." *Black Sheep Newsletter,* Spring/Summer 1975, Issue 3/4.

-----. "Summary of Spurlock Projects Up to Fall, 1974." *Black Sheep Newsletter,* Winter 1978, Issue 25.

COLORED WOOL PUBLICATIONS

Black Baa. Black and Coloured Sheep Breeders' Association of New Zealand. Sue Stewart, "Kahurangi", R.D. 4, Masterton, New Zealand.

Black Sheep Newsletter. Sachiye Jones, 28068 Ham Road, Eugene, Oregon 97405.

Breeding Coloured Sheep and Using Coloured Wool. Papers presented at the National Congress, Adelaide, South Australia, January 30-February 3, 1979. Peacock Publishers, Frewville, South Australia, Australia.

The Marker. Natural Colored Wool Growers Association. Cliff Cain, Star Route, Box 48, Brooks, California 95606.

THINKING OF ANNE

BY LILLIAN ELLIOTT AND PAT HICKMAN

It seems completely appropriate that I should write a photo essay for a book in honor of Anne Blinks. Ever since I first met Anne, I have introduced friends to her; this is a new way to introduce her to others. All of us who write in this book have been deeply touched by Anne, her thinking, her work, her life. We return the compliment by giving her what we have on the subjects closest to our hearts, often having been stimulated in our own individual directions by Anne's own interests. She has accepted each of us as we are, sensitive to our differences, sometimes amused by them, sharing herself with us.   —L.

Anne puts up with that which we don't completely understand, delighting in showing what her mind — with its love of complexities and complicated structures — has "figured out."   —P.

Half the pleasure for Anne in understanding something is in being able to show it and share it with others.   —L.

After a day with her, one falls into bed exhausted from straining to take in absolutely the total experience of her creative, curious mind.   —P.

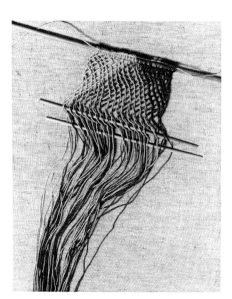

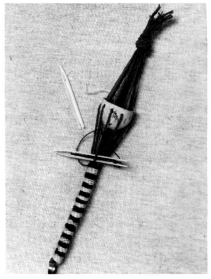

There are heaps and piles in Anne's studio—the most exciting clutter one can imagine. What disappears, seemingly buried under books and papers, bits and pieces of "rags", is bound to resurface—a challenge, an unanswered question, an ongoing "game".

—P.

I have always been impressed by Anne's direct way with animals; they want so to please her. To see the bond between her and the various dogs she has raised has been a rare privilege. Her sheep, too, come when she calls. Anne smiles and claims it's because she says "Please."

—L.

Anne is so educated. She calls to mind and tongue phrases of classic literature, wonderfully apt at that precise moment. The classics, like the animals, come at her bidding.

—L.

And there is such pleasure in books, in friends who recognize what she has to give.

—P.

Sheep without Anne seems much less interesting. Her own, naturally, run from strangers, but when they see her coming, they gather 'round, wanting to be petted, individually called by name, given attention.   —P.

There are sounds of sheep
bells, of tree frogs.　　　—P.

Yet another puzzle, a brief unkown, eagerly awaiting Anne's inventive solution.   —P.

From years of careful looking, of work at it, Anne understands, and if she doesn't, she works harder at it. There is admiration for another weaver's expertise. Anne brings new life to pre-Columbian textiles as she handles them with such regard.   —P.

Anne knows two ways anywhere, the scenic route, and the food path. She knows the best food available, where to buy it, and how to prepare it; and one of the real pleasures in life is eating with Anne.   —L.

It is difficult in today's society for people of different ages to become friends. How wonderful to have to run to keep up with a woman twenty years older, and to admire her quick mind. As I've come to know and appreciate Anne it has made my own growing older a little easier.   —L.

It is such a gift to be able to spend time with Anne Blinks.
                    —P.

Photos in "Thinking Of Anne" by:
Sally Blinks, Lillian Elliott, Leslie
Grace, Terry Gritton, Pat Hickman,
and Linda Ligon.